HIGHBALL

A PAGEANT OF TRAINS

C. M. Clegg

MAIN-LINE MIKADO ON THE MIDLAND VALLEY

The motive power of the Midland Valley, the Kansas, Oklahoma and Gulf and the Oklahoma City-Ada-Atoka Railway Companies maintaining a network of freight and passenger service between Wichita and Arkansas City, Kansas, Tulsa, Muskogee, and Oklahoma City, Oklahoma, and Denison, Texas, bear their entire corporate titles on their car herald and caboose insignia. Locomotives, however, are simply initialed M. V., and their roster is possessed of some of the handsomest and best tended engines in the Southwest. Here is M. V. No. 93, a well-shopped Mikado with a tender tank attached, rolling a short cut of high cars eastward at Carpenter's Bluff, Texas, with a full head of steam and safety valves popping.

HIGHBALL

A PAGEANT OF TRAINS

by LUCIUS BEEBE

BONANZA BOOKS • NEW YORK

This edition published by Bonanza Books,
distributed by Crown Publishers, Inc.,
by arrangement with Hawthorn Properties,
a division of E.P. Dutton, Inc.

Manufactured in the United States of America

Library of Congress Cataloging in Publication Data
Beebe, Lucius Morris, 1902–1966.
    Highball, a pageant of trains.
    Reprint. Originally published: New York:
D. Appleton-Century, 1945.
    1. Railroads—United States.   2. Railroads—
United States—Trains.   I. Title.
TF23.B38   1982   385′.0973   82-12975

ISBN: 0-517-004208
v u t s r q

HIGHBALL: Railroad parlance for a clearance, clear track, or order to proceed, deriving from the metal globes by which train movements were controlled before the introduction of semaphores or other position signals.

Lucius Beebe

CONTENTS

Lucius Beebe

ILLUSTRATIONS

C. M. Clegg

INTRODUCTION

IT IS the hope of the author of this book that whatever readers it may encounter will not seek in its editorial economy a definitive volume on American railroading, still less a comprehensive survey of the practices and mystery of the high iron. As a matter of factual record, *Highball* has been written and photographed in the expectation that it may form an integral part of a somewhat larger picture of railroading when viewed as complementary to its antecedent volumes, *High Iron*, *Highliners*, and *Trains in Transition*, and that, considered together, the four books may constitute a reasonable coverage of some aspects of a highly specialized and at the same time widely diffused subject.

Any single subdivision of the subject of railroading—its history, motive power, operations technique, finance, and legend, even its literature, music, and ballad lore—is in itself suitable material for many books. Even so monumental and impressive a work as Dollfus and Geoffroy's *Histoire de la locomotion terrestre*, perhaps the most authoritative railroad history yet evolved, strains to contain its subject in a single and beautiful volume.

Highball, like its companion pieces, has been brought into being in the full knowledge that profound change is at hand in the shops and roundhouses and dispatchers' offices of the countryside and that, indeed, many of the most fascinating chapters of the legend must already be written in the past tense. The Taunton-built locomotives of the sixties and seventies, many of the narrow-gage and short lines, with happy and ambitious beginnings and the wonderful variety and gaudy pattern of passenger travel of only yesterday, are already with *"les neiges d'antan"* of the Villon poem, and the would-be historian must be pat and avid to seize upon all the glamour that is left to the rails if he is to preserve any part of it for the dreary and Diesel-shrouded future. He may weep that no single railroad photographer of the eighties possessed a modern speed camera, but he must also be quick to realize that even the color and charm still left to railroading may not be available to the historian of tomorrow or the day after.

There is still, as this is written, gaily varnished rolling stock in the uplands of Colorado and Nevada, and sleek, high-wheeled Atlantic type locomotives yet power the short hauls on many a Pennsy's dispatch sheet which in a decade may have disappeared, from active service at least, as completely as the Sharp's rifle, the Saratoga trunk, and the Amoskeag steam fire engine. No Hamlet ever demanded of Horatio his tablets—"My tables,—meet it is I set it down . . ."—more urgently than the chronicler of American railroading should call for his Speed Graphic and film of fastest emulsion speed.

The world is obviously the poorer that the fine flowering of the overland stage coach, the Mississippi River steamer, and the packets and clipper ships of an even earlier period were not known to the recording devices of photography. Even the fascinating machine mentioned above, the Amoskeag fire pumper, drawn by three splendid horses and an almost daily familiar in the lives of Americans up to thirty-odd years ago, is represented by an almost unbelievable poverty of material in the files of the great photographic agencies. Many of the most casual properties of only the last generation, Stoughton Bitters, congress gaiters, the Remington derringer, Florida water, the Pinsch gaslight, still linger in the language but evoke no imagined or tangible quality.

For the recording of the Concord coach and the Allaire walking beam of the sidewheeler, lithography, painting, and the written word are admired and admirable mediums, but they are not factual, documentary, and explicit in the sense that the arrested photographic image is these things. Railroading is the first great evolutionary manifestation of man's imagining to be born coeval with the photographic camera, and whose technical developments have been nicely paced to the perfecting of the instrument of its record. There was no Folmer patent Graflex with a potential speed of 1/1,000 second when, in 1848, the world's first mile-a-minute speed was achieved by the Boston and Maine's immortal Antelope on the Boston-Lawrence haul, but, forty-five years later, when the Empire State Express made history with its 112.5 miles an hour, the practice of action photography was sufficiently advanced to record the Central's 999 at speed over the track pans at Poughkeepsie and to preserve its style and the pride of its going for all time.

The function and office of the railroad historian are difficult of definition, since his subject matter requires exposition rather than interpretation and, unlike so many aspects of history, demands little orientation to other parallel aspects of the record. The saga of steam and overland steel is largely self-contained, self-evident, and self-sufficient. Its operations are almost wholly devoid of figures and personalities. The most vivid and colorful characters to emerge from the American railroading saga of the nineteenth century were not so much Jack Casement, William Mason, or Theodore Judah as they were the scoundrelly capitalists of Wall Street and Nob Hill in black broadcloth tailcoats and General Grant whiskers. It was the Commodore Vanderbilts, Leland Stanfords, and Daniel Drews who have proved such fearsome fellows in the biographies written by men who, in their own proper lifetimes, never quite paid off the mortgage on the house.

The closest approximation to honesty in any writer of consequence remarking on the great princes of the rails was achieved by Ambrose Bierce who, one San Francisco morning in the nineties, was observed by a friend to be speculatively, even longingly, eyeing the fine swinging doors of Flood and O'Brien's Saloon in Sutter Street.

"There," sighed the noisiest crusader against vested corruption of his generation, "there, lapped in luxury and upholstered in Babylonish devisings, sipping rare vintages of great cost and plotting further brigandage against a toiling people, are those arch-thieves and conscienceless pillagers, Leland Stanford, Charles Crocker, Mark Hopkins, and Collis Huntington. Even now, no doubt, they scheme to loot more outrageously than ever the people and commonwealth of California! I wish I might be one of them!"

The fascinations and romance of railroading are almost altogether implicit in specialized mechanical function, the complex integrated agencies which find their fulfillment in steel wheels rolling over vast, meticulously channeled distances. Tracks, motive power, and rolling stock, and to a somewhat less degree their coördination and control through human agencies supply the enchantments of rail transport. The railroad *aficionado* is prone to supply his own element of personality to the art and mystery he cultivates when he endows a locomotive with attributes of animation, speaking of it fondly, as with ships, in the feminine gender rather than the more strictly justified neuter.

The borrowed time on which a vast number of little railroads have been living is, as this is being written, coming to a close. The end of the wars and the restoration of competition in the field of transport, both of passengers and of merchandise, must inevitably spell the end of many short lines in the Deep South and Middle West. There is, however, an amazing and heartening vitality to the business of railroading and business is being and will in some cases probably continue indefinitely to be done over some of the most improbable-appearing properties. The author and his associate lay in wait one recent summer evening beside the twin, but scarcely ever parallel, streaks of rust they knew to be the main and only line of the Virginia and Carolina Southern, a feeder of the Seaboard Air Line, near Lumberton, North Carolina. The adjustment of his camera to 1/200 second seemed approximately as optimistic as the loading of an elephant rifle in Times Square. Surely no motive power or consist more ponderous than a OO scale model could maintain itself on these travesty rails which stretched casually through the southern woodlands, overgrown with grass and shrubs, innocent of fish plates and in many places of ties themselves where the original wood had again merged with the elemental earth! But sure enough, just before dusk a gentle sighing sound came across the distant meadow, and a train swam slowly toward us through the tall grass. It was a beautiful and wonderful train advancing with an elaboration of caution under a cloud of undulant soot, like some aged beldame in a wreath of widow's weeds. Its capped-stack locomotive combined extreme elegance with imponderable age. Its half a dozen high cars swayed and dipped over the almost nonexistent iron in an ecstasy of improbability. The rolling shanty that was its caboose was peopled with happy Negroes, one of them possessed, as though he had been secured from some celestial casting agency, with an indignant sort of fiddle. The Negroes sang, very low and no two the same song. The rear shack beat time with his brakeman's club and on the final platform was a crate of red-combed fowl whose life prospect, as they rattled toward some darktown dinner table, seemed very poor indeed.

It was a train out of heaven, a train such as a little boy might draw with uncertain crayons in his sketch book, and yet the Virginia and Carolina Southern is a valuable property. It owns three locomotives, each more elaborately obsolete than the next. It has no dispatchers and, indeed, not even a telephone between its stations. Passengers may ride among the darkies in the caboose and the freight agent knows when the daily train is coming by its smoke against the sky. But every year it provides many hundreds of carloads of tobacco, cotton, and lumber for the A.C.L. and is strictly a going concern. The management is muttering about Diesels.

More, however, even than locomotives, individual railroads themselves incline to recommend their personalities to human sentimentality and to assume characteristics quite divorced from the tangible resources assigned them in their corporate articles. To the considered judgment the Missouri-Kansas-Texas or, say, the Chicago and Eastern Illinois cannot in any way bear comparison with the vast and glittering transcontinental systems, the Santa Fe, the Union Pacific, the Burlington. And yet, to many and many an imagining, it is a railroad of secondary economic importance, a narrow-gage or short line that has a close hold on the heart, is freighted with wonder and delight because of some sentimental association, a circumstance of motive power, or an accident of geography in the terrain it serves.

It so happens that, to the author, there are some all but obsolete high-wheel Atlantic type passenger engines on the Cotton Belt, some right-of-way vistas along the Gulf, Mobile, and Ohio, the ageless elms arching above the meadow sidings of the Bellefonte Central, the hours of departure between ten and noon at the old Dearborn Station in Chicago, and a now doubtless decommissioned dining car of ancient splendors on the Fort Worth and Denver City which have no equal in their counterparts elsewhere. The cult of antiquity and obsolescence for their own sake is not an entirely vital one, but there are sensibilities which recoil from the meretricious fraudulences of airflow design and the sullen secrecies of Diesel-electric power.

And there are still evidences of the storied and immemorial legend of railroading in the years of its flowery magnificence: the highball arms of the crossover signals of the St. Louis Southwestern in the rice lands of Arkansas; the brave canary yellow coaches of the Virginia & Truckee, peopled with the ghosts of Flood and Fair and Mackay; the covered bridges of the St. Johnsbury and Lake Champlain. The past beats against them as the night wind against a storm lantern; the urgency of their preservation in some form is as compulsive as a 31 order over a single circuit in the snow-bound High Sierras. Their import and symbolism is that of Stephen Benét's "riders shaking the heart with the hooves that will not cease," and they stand as reminders still of heroic times in the land. And they are one with placer diggings and the Jingle Bob, the hallmarks of California and the Chisum steer, the C.C. on the minted gold of Carson City, the Wells Fargo scales, the Conestoga wagon and the Starr's Navy pistol, all the identifications and styles, the devices and coat armor of a way of living as vanished as the longhorn and as distinctive as Medford rum.

I have hoped to preserve a little of them for the record.

———

For assistance in the preparation of this book the author is indebted in varying degrees to several persons beside the contributing photographers to whom credit is assigned, and he prayerfully hopes correctly, along with their pictures in the text. His paramount obligation is to his technical associate and companion on safari in far places, Charles M. Clegg, who has shared with him many dubious nights' lodgings in west Texas, the gelid altitudes of Colorado, the wartime insolences of minor officiousness, and the underproof whisky which universally besets the wanderer from his native and accustomed deadfalls. He has encountered with equanimity motor car failure on Wolf Creek Pass in dead of winter and the infamies of wartime menus on the Pennsylvania; and a study of his photographs in this book will reveal a devotion to the atmosphere and wonder of railroading not often encountered.

The author acknowledges, too, courtesies and sometimes courtliness on the part of President William M. Jeffers of the Union Pacific, President Daniel Upthegrove of the Cotton Belt, and President Matthew Sloan of the Katy, as well as Volney Fowler of the Electro Motive Corporation, E. A. West of the Rio Grande, Russel Coulter of the Frisco, M. L. Lyles of the Santa Fe, and the editors of *Trains, Railway Age,* and

Railroad Magazine. President J. J. Pelley of the Association of American Railroads has used his good and powerful offices whenever various railroad officials of exasperating or military turn of minds have objected to the photographing of their property. There are times when the railroad historian, be he never so well accredited, must combat not alone the weather, the dispatchers' schedules, and other acts of God, but also the operating departments and vice-nobodies of the very railroads he would endeavor to lend some fractional yet fragrant immortality. The author is, too, obligated to Miss Ina T. Aulls of the Western Collection of the Denver Public Library for the most generous research and coöperation in the field of Colorado antiquities; to Jerry Arzrouni of the Eastman Kodak Company of New York, whose unfailing interest in the author's photographic projects made them possible at a time when such undertakings could be compassed only with the most authoritative assistance; and to H. I. Phillips and the New York *Sun* for permission to reprint in Chapter 6 his verses, "The Glorified Caboose."

For those who have helped him in this essay, the author wishes that fortune may ever give them a clear board, and he salutes them: Highball!

L. B.

Lucius Beebe

1
SOME LITTLE RAILROADS

THE year 1888, in the world and the United States in general, and in and around New York City in particular, was freighted with nervous excitements. The eastern seaboard had at length dug itself out of the drifts occasioned by the great blizzard which will forever be known by the year of its occurrence, and Chester Conklin had succumbed to pneumonia occasioned by falling in a snowdrift during the record fall. The Metropolitan Opera Company of New York, in an era when boiled shirts and diamond tiaras were the outward and visible symbols not alone of respectability but also of social achievement, was vastly concerned over whether or not to include German opera in its season's repertoire. The German Kaiser was annoyed with France and was shaking a noisy saber in its scabbard.

The columns of the New York *Daily Tribune* were occupied by advertisements for Jaeckel the furrier's latest importation, a "seal Parisian walking jacket," and a patent nostrum against pneumonia called Denison's Plaster whose typeset read ominously: "Paraded Saturday, Died Monday!" The West still maintained a profound hold upon the public imagination and *Century Magazine*'s frontier article for November was entitled "Looking for Camp." Classified advertisements of coachmen and grooms seeking employment occupied half a column of agate type in the New York *Herald*.

In the world of railroading, too, brave doings were toward. A newly financed and organized road, the Ridgefield and New York Railroad Company, was laying track from Danbury, Connecticut, to New York City with an eye, doubtless, to making the celebrated Danbury Fair as well as the hat building resources of that city more immediately accessible to Manhattan. Throughout New York state the car stove had been forbidden by law in all passenger equipment, and railroad executives were shaking dubious heads over the expense of installing steam pipes in the wooden, open-platform rolling stock of their properties. The Pennsylvania announced a five per cent dividend on its common stock, a half of one per cent less than in 1887, but the market bore up bravely under the intelligence. In Chicago, the Lake Shore and Michigan Southern Company was having sharp words with the Chicago and Western Indiana and filed a bill to restrain the latter road from interfering with the business of laying Lake Shore iron across the tracks of the C. & W. I. to join the main line of the Rock Island at Chicago Heights.

And across the New Jersey meadows, from New Brunswick to South Amboy, Irish graders and track gangs were laying the fills and light iron for what promised to be much more than a mere connecting railroad if ever the tracks of what was then as now known as the Raritan River Railroad should extend far enough across the main line of the Pennsylvania to join at Bound Brook with the far-reaching systems of the Lehigh Valley, the Baltimore and Ohio, the Central Railroad of New Jersey, and the Reading Company. Had this ambitious plan been realized it is possible that the vast quantity of industrial freight now syphoned out of South Amboy by the Pennsylvania might have been diverted to other roads through the agency of the Raritan River and the ambitious little project have ended as a through-haul carrier in its own right. Legal and financial difficulties, however, limited the Raritan River essentially to the trackage, completed in 1890, between South Amboy and New Brunswick, with spurs to Sayreville, Amclay, and the lead mines and docks that lie adjacent to the Raritan River itself just around the bend to Perth Amboy and the glistening reaches of Raritan Bay.

Time, however, has dealt more gently with the Raritan than it has with many another short connecting line and today this little pike, about twelve miles in length, operating without signals on telephonic dispatching and with a motive power roster of only eight steam locomotives, is very much a going concern and the last example of big-time railroading and the grand manner of the high iron in minuscule within easy distance of New York City. It is standard-gage; its engines are more modern than many and many a valitudinarian kettle still in service along the main lines of the Wabash, C. & E. I., and Monon, and the sight of No. 5, a flange-stacked Baldwin 2-8-2 built in 1910, double-heading with No. 11 at the head end of forty high cars and No. 7 pushing from behind as they breast the grade of Bergen Hill is a picture to quicken the pulses and lift the railroading heart. The morning mists of Raritan Bay are shivered with their advance, the high stacks thunder with their exhaust, the coupled locomotives roll and shudder perilously over the light iron, the heavy consist glides by, the caboose and rear helper vanish again into the absorbent fog, and there has come and gone a vision of railroading as true and authentic as any sight of the Union Pacific's ponderous Mallets fighting for life on Sherman Hill a few miles west of Cheyenne.

The destinies of the Raritan are minor and homely destinies involved with brick kilns, coalyards and pie factories. A momentary touch of terror and grandeur, perhaps, derives from the traffic stemming from the vast du Pont-Hercules explosive manufactury at Parlin and another du Pont subsidiary which manufactures cinema films hard by, and for these perilous chores No. 11 has had its stack fitted with an eye-filling spark arrester. But mostly the road's business is with lumberyards, pigmented clays, and the delivery of tank cars to the Texas Company at Milltown. The Raritan's last passenger revenue, in the sum of $92, was earned in 1938. It once carried some 9,000 commuters weekly in its passenger and mixed trains, and handsome stone and brick stations at Parlin and New Brunswick testify to its prosperity as a passenger road only a few years ago. Today the station at Parlin houses an orderly and well-staffed freight bureau and business office. The sightly little depot at the New Brunswick terminal has closed its waiting room and boarded up its open fireplace, but its freight house is in good repair, and in the station agent's office a battery of telephones, filing cases, and calendars, torn to the current month, from the Minneapolis & St. Louis Railroad show it to be a going concern.

Very much as is the scheme of things on the West Shore branch of the New York Central, where all westbound traffic is dispatched by day and trains headed for New York run by night, the local freights of the Raritan set out from South Amboy, where they have been made up during the night in the classification yards of the New York and Long Branch and the Pennsylvania, and roll westward during the morning hours. In the late afternoon the train crews pick up eastbound cars from New Brunswick, Milltown, South River, Vandeventer, Gillespie, and Parlin, from Sayreville Junction and Phoenix, and rest for the night in the home roundhouse at South Amboy. No. 5 is the oldest engine in continuous service on the Raritan and was the second No. 5 on its roster. The first No. 5, however, is merely a legend, shrouded in mystery. All that anyone remembers is that it was a 4-4-0 American type locomotive—quite the lady, but her origins and her end are obscure. Just how a full-size steam locomotive could disappear or be scrapped without a trace and leave behind it no record of its going on the company books baffles H. Filskov, chief operations officer, but that's all anybody knows nowadays. Its most modern motive power is No. 7, an 0-6-0 switcher built by Baldwin in 1919 and purchased by the Raritan from the Chattahoochee Valley a few years later. Altogether the Raritan has stabled twenty-one steamers in its roundhouse since 1890 and nowadays it makes a practice of keeping seven engines in daily operation and one in the backshops at all times.

The right-of-way of the little road, for the most part, is over New Jersey meadows and fresh ponds and inlets from the tidal reaches of the Raritan River. There is a stiff grade through a lonely woodland cut, in fall thickly populated by hunters, just east of Milltown. Deserted spurs and moldering factory premises testify that once this stretch was alive with small industrial projects, gravel pits, manufactories, and agricultural undertakings. At South River the single iron passes over desolate marshes and spans a curving arm of water within sight of the domed spires of the town's Orthodox Russian Church. At Parlin there are comparatively spacious switching yards, a water tower of ancient brick and wooden design, and a protected grade crossing, while a few miles farther on, the line crosses the tremendous sand pits and narrow-gage railroad system of a cement and gravel works. At no time, save perhaps in the deep woods of Milltown, are the train crews of the Raritan out of sight of the tall smokestacks and factory sites of industry, but even so, the illusion persists that it is primarily a country railroad, a rural enterprise serving the necessities of suburban existence.

The Raritan is, of course, the result of many and varied antecedent circumstances in the history of New Jersey railroading. The region it serves is an old one, industrially speaking, and a century and more ago the cargo boats and passenger packets from Philadelphia went up the

Delaware River to Trenton and so inland by way of the Delaware and Raritan Canal to reach tidewater again at New Brunswick. This pattern was broken by the construction of the storied Camden and Amboy Railroad, now a part of the Pennsylvania system. A clue to the ownership and management of the Raritan River Railroad may be found in the person of its chief officer and vice-president who is George LeBoutillier, executive of the Pennsylvania Railroad, but the Raritan is still proud in its own motive power, its own herald on its shiny red, double-truck cabooses, and the legend of its own separate and individual entity lettered in gold on the tenders of its locomotives which buck and heave valiantly ahead of thirty- and forty-car trains over its twelve miles of main-line iron. Any inquiry into the internal economy of the Raritan River will disclose that it is financially profitable, both as an individual enterprise and as an agency for the collection and distribution of revenue freight for the Pennsylvania, whose South Amboy extension meets the mighty mainline at that crossroads of the railroad world, Monmouth Junction. But more than this it is a homely and familiar factor in the daily lives of the communities it serves and one which no other agency of transport is likely to supplant in the immediate future. Buses and private motor cars have absorbed its passenger traffic, but it is improbable that trucks can, with economy and profit, handle its not inconsiderable bulk of lumber, sand, coal, and other non-perishable merchandise.

The Raritan River is the archetypal connecting railroad, the dream railroad out of only yesterday. Its disintegrating ties, sometimes laid in eccentric patterns, its archaically light rails and original fluted fishplates laid down more than half a century ago, its hand operated switches and homely informality of dispatching are redolent of wistful railroading years, and it would surprise almost nobody if some morning No. 11 should come muttering down the grade from Phoenix with a bearded engineer in a curly derby hat leaning out of the driver's side. Its rolling stock (except its brightly lacquered cabooses) bears the car heralds of other railroads; the platforms of its passenger stations are peopled with commuting ghosts; enthusiastic huntsmen have riddled the warning signs at its grade crossings. But there is fire, metaphorically and factually, in its boilers; the main and connecting rods clatter and are instinct with life; on the high (and only) iron of the Raritan River there is traffic still.

The Raritan River with its almost irreducibly short mileage and well shopped stable of little locomotives is, to be sure, only one of a multitude of short-haul railroads, each an individual entity, a personality to the sentimental, a microcosm of the vast industry of railroading to the more precise-minded.

Consider now the Wichita Falls & Southern Railroad Company which operates over 170 miles of something less than well-ballasted iron bearing the railmark "Carnegie 1898" almost 2,000 miles from the tidewater meadows of New Jersey. The Wichita Falls runs between the town of that name in north Texas almost on the Oklahoma boundary, and Dublin, Texas, on an almost north and south axis. During its progress over the hilly landscape its principal stations are located at Breckenridge, Breckwalker, Ringling Junction, and Ranger, at the last of which points it connects with the vast, wealthy Texas and Pacific and crosses the T. & P. main line at a neat right angle. There are three trains each way every week, mixed, and although it runs through a region of opulent natural resources, mostly oil, and is possessed of a misleadingly neat and modern station and freight house at Breckenridge, to say that the Wichita Falls & Southern were well-to-do would be an excess of optimism. It has, however, if not rich relatives, at least rich connections, at Dublin with the Katy, at Graham with the Rock Island, and with the aforementioned T. & P. at Ranger. At Wichita Falls, too, it exchanges cars with the Fort Worth and Denver City, but at Breckwalker its switching operations with the Eastland, Wichita Falls & Gulf are only a happy memory. This last little road was torn up late in 1944.

Stand in a windy pasture filled with Texas shorthorn steers about to head for the slaughter houses of Fort Worth on a spring day and watch the erratic progress of No. 44 northbound over the varying grades at noontime. At times the billowing smoke plume moves with amazing speed, at times appears almost static, and a closer scrutiny of its approach reveals that the consist of fifteen tanks and stock cars moves very rapidly on the downslopes, very slowly indeed on the grades. As it comes abreast it may be seen that its power is No. 30, a 2-8-0 veteran of the early twenties whose clattering side rods and clouds of steam escaping from cylinder heads suggest that shopping is a comparatively rare luxury.

C. M. Clegg

WORKING STEAM ON BERGEN HILL

Nearing the summit of Bergen Hill in a deep cut on the outskirts of South Amboy, the Raritan's first eastbound train of the day, with No. 9 on the smoky end and No. 7, a 0-6-0 switcher, behind the caboose, out of sight around the curve, rocks uphill at a ponderous five miles an hour. When there are forty cars in a train consist on this grade the superintendent of motive power calls out four engines, two head end and two behind, to hike the heavy freight up the grade.

C. M. Clegg

Lucius Beebe

"LOOK, THEY'RE TAKING OUR PICTURE!"

The head-end crew of No. 5 crowds to the fireman's gangway to see the excitement as the shutters click. With the helper on the rear still working steam to clear the summit of Bergen Hill, No. 5 on the head end is running free on the down grade with valves popping and just a wisp of steam condensing in the cold winter air of New Jersey. The swing shack and parlor man, obviously, are having a mug-up of coffee in the caboose in preference to decorating the car tops in this weather.

THE FIVE SPOT HAULS
ITS TONNAGE

The Raritan River's No. 5 with a string of twenty cars, seven of them empty tanks from the Sinclair Refining plant at New Brunswick, clatters over the switch points in the yards a mile or so down the track from Parlin, heading for the home terminal at the end of a long day setting out cars along the railroad's busy right-of-way. No. 5's flanged stack is unique on the power roster of the Raritan and until recently it carried a standard pilot where now there are footboards. No. 11, shown below, boasts a fancy bonnet in the form of a spark arrester on its stack.

Lucius Beebe

"OH! WHAT A BEAUTIFUL MORNIN'!"

With the frost from the night before still silver on the sixty-pound rails and the Jersey uplands shorn of all but their final leaves, No. 9 whistles boldly for a grade crossing as the engineer notches his throttle for the westward run from the Amboys and Raritan Bay to the sleepy college town of New Brunswick, the western terminal of the line. Oil, lumber, and merchandise are in her mixed freight, and on busy days the Raritan River rolls as many as a hundred cars off the connecting tracks of the New York and Long Branch and the Pennsylvania for distribution along the way.

Courtesy of Railroad Magazine

A WOOD-BURNER IN THE DEEP SOUTH

Train No. 1 of the seventy-six-mile wood-burning Live Oak, Perry & Gulf Railroad rolls carefully across a timber trestle at the edge of the famed Suwanee River near Live Oak, Florida.

Lucius Beebe

SUNSET ON THE RAILS

For thirty years the Raritan River's No. 9, a gracefully turned Mikado with a tall, straight stack and rakish pilot, has banged and pounded over the road's light iron, breasted the grade on Bergen Hill, rolled easily over the salt marshes of South River, clattered over the switch points of Parlin and Sayreville Junction. Baldwin-built and neither in its first youth nor extreme senescence, as motive power goes, No. 9 is archetypal of the locomotives of connecting lines before the Diesels came. Here, at sunset on a September day, against a woodland background, it is climbing the grade out of Milltown, with a full head of steam and an exhaust rolling up against the New Jersey sky, headed for the roundhouse at South Amboy for the night. There are seven cars in the train's consist, with an old high car serving as crummy.

Lucius Beebe

VIGNETTE OF OLD-TIME RAILROADING

Here are the essential properties of a railroad: motive power, train consist, double tracks for passing and switching operations and a switch leading to the house track, switch signals, a water tower and a rural background. To complete the picture all that is lacking are main-line signals, a round house, and turntable. The scene is at Parlin as No. 9, westbound, has finished setting out its cars for this station, and is gathering way for the run to South River, Milltown, and New Brunswick.

C. M. Clegg

LITTLE GIANT RAILROAD

The trackage of the Lehigh & Hudson River Railway from Easton, Pennsylvania, to Maybrook, New York, is only eighty-five miles, most of it through rural and woodland New Jersey. But while it is justifiable to consider the L. & H. R. a "little railroad," it is still a vital and heavily traveled link between industrial Pennsylvania and lower New England where it connects with the New Haven. Its power roster boasts several Mikados of more tonnage capacity and modern design than this Consolidation, but no engine could make a finer picture of country operations than No. 93 hitting a fast seventy over the heavily ballasted track at Great Meadows, New Jersey.

C. M. Clegg

A NARROW-GAGE YARDS IN DEEPEST PENNSYLVANIA

Complete and in miniature are the yards and shops of the strait-gage East Broad Top Railroad at Orbisonia, Pennsylvania, and the photograph shows its heavy-weight slim-gage rail, stub switches, and target switch stands, relics from the railroading past of other times. Several of the road's ten wooden coaches and four combines are shown spotted for the "Miners' Special" which rolls between Orbisonia and the Broad Top coal mines when they are in operation.

KEEPING UP WITH THE PROCESSION

Upper left:
C. M. Clegg

With No. 9 on the head end of a cut of fifteen high cars, tanks, and gondolas, fighting up Bergen Hill, an added inducement to progress takes the form of No. 14, fresh from the shops and gleaming in a fresh coat of glossy black paint with gold trim. In more conventional railroad practice the helper engine would be cut in ahead of the caboose, but in the case of the Raritan's No. 6 crummy, which has a steel underframe, this precaution is not necessary.

A SHORT-LINE RAILROAD WITH BIG-TIME TRAFFIC

Lower left:
D. W. Yungneyer,
Courtesy of Trains

The Detroit and Mackinac Railroad owns 240-odd miles of track and there are some of its divisions where heavy passenger trains still roll, but it generally ranks as a short line, and here is No. 116, a tall-stacked Mogul running out of Omer, Michigan, with a special and one of the D. & M.'s own high cars behind the tender and enough smoke exhaust to give the vapors to the operating department.

C. M. Clegg

WEATHERFORD, MINERAL WELLS & NORTHWESTERN

"AFFABLE LIVE-OAK, LEANING LOW"

Sidney Lanier

The dense woodland of the New Jersey countryside at Gainesburgh Junction, five miles east of the Delaware Water Gap, provides a sylvan and unaccustomed setting for one of the Lehigh & New England's powerful consolidations with tender boosters headed east with a long drag of coal from the Pennsylvania mines. Over this portion of the main line of this coal-haul road the high iron is hidden for miles in the dense green of summer woods which lends a sense of unreality to the thundering passage of the heavy tonnage of big-time industry.

C. M. Clegg

"THERE ARE TRACES OF AGE IN THE ONE-HOSS SHAY
A GENERAL FLAVOR OF MILD DECAY."

Oliver Wendell Holmes.

A valetudinarian ark, painted a weathered green and creaking in its progress across the Pennsylvania countryside, is the passenger equipment of the Bellefonte Central, which accommodates paying patrons on its daily round trip from Belle-fonte to State College by way of Fillmore, Krumrine and Waddle. It is notable that the motive power of the Bellefonte Central is not only of less heroic vintage but also more lovingly shopped, conditioned, and maintained.

"DEEP SHADES IN THE HILLS OF HABERSHAM,
THESE GLADES IN THE VALLEYS OF HALL."

Sidney Lanier.

Right: Lucius Beebe

Neither the hills of Habersham nor the glades in the valley of Hall which so took the fancy of Sidney Lanier actually appear on the time card of the Bellefonte Central Railroad, but its shaded woodlands with their arching tall trees and its meadowlands and streams might well engage the attentions of the lyric muse. Here its daily mixed train from Bellefonte to State College rounds the bend at Horseshoe Curve deep in the Pennsylvania Hills as No. 19 blasts the summer afternoon with its rhythmic exhaust on the westbound run.

AN EIGHT-WHEELER STEPS OUT IN STYLE

Compared to multiple-motored units of Diesel-electric motive power costing in excess of $500,000, the $12,275 which the directors of the Huntingdon and Broad Top Mountain spent for No. 30 in 1907 seems relatively trivial, and yet one pauses to wonder how many of today's Diesel monsters will be in active service thirty-five years hence. At one time No. 30 was placed in storage while the road tried out a gas-electric coach which promptly wrecked itself beyond repair, and No. 30 was reinstated over the road's passenger hauls out of Huntingdon where it is shown with a milk car, a coach, and a combined baggage-mail car running south into the Pennsylvania hills on the nine o'clock morning scheduled haul.

TO AQUASHICOLA, TO KUNKLETOWN, TO WALKTON

A rare collector's item is the Chestnut Ridge Railroad the greater part of whose traffic is within the limits of Palmerton, Pennsylvania, a community of forges, furnaces, and heavy industry, but once a day a local freight sets out for Kunkletown, twenty-two miles up the shady valley that rolls beside Chestnut Ridge itself. Its right-of-way rambles wonderfully beside trout streams, covered bridges, and sleepy settlements with fine Dutch brick churches. The semaphore signals at the depot in Little Gap give an approximate indication of the naïve delights of this back-country railroad. Above is one of the Chestnut Ridge's eight-wheelers emerging from the smoky premises of the New Jersey Zinc Company of Pennsylvania.

At right: a clear board on the Chestnut Ridge.

C. M. Clegg

GHOST TRAIN TO YESTERDAY

Outranking in the fragrance of bonanza times and the spacious days of the Comstock Lode all other railroads living and dead is the famed Virginia & Truckee, which, in its heyday, carried the inestimable wealth of Gold Hill and Virginia City to the bank vaults of San Francisco. Today the V. & T. owns but three steam locomotives, the rest having gone to museums or the films, and its daily run is between Reno, Carson City, and Minden, but once fifty daily trains were scheduled for Mound House and Virginia City. Then its overnight sleepers to San Francisco were peopled with golden names: William Sharon, William Ralston, Darius O. Mills, Adolph Sutro, and the Irish bonanza kings: Fair, Mackay, Flood, and O'Brien. The V. & T. enjoyed a complete monopoly of Nevada gold and silver and on occasion its proprietors divided $100,000 a month in dividends, while it has been estimated that, during the golconda years, the V. & T. hauled from the mines its own weight in silver, including the tonnage of every rail, tie, trestle, car, and locomotive. Today the International Hotel, Virginia City's great caravansery with the first elevator in the west, is a gaudy memory; the Crystal Chandeliers Saloon is but a museum of the stupendous past; Piper's Opera House a clapboard ruin haunted by memories of President Grant, General Sherman, and George Pullman. But the valiant little yellow and green Kimball cars, themselves dating from the seventies, still connect with the Southern Pacific night and morning at Reno and flash spiritedly over the light iron at Washoe, Steamboat, and Ophir, their principal freight the non-revenue memories of the transcendent past, of gold and empire and the West.

Lucius Beebe

OTIUM CUM DIGNITATE

C. M. Clegg

The Virginia & Truckee Railroad was just beginning when this construction car, built in its own shops at Carson City, in 1869, first rolled over the newly laid fifty- and sixty-pound rails of William Sharon's bonanza pike. The first passenger equipment, built by the Kimball Manufacturing Company of San Francisco, had not yet been hauled over the High Sierras for service on the new Nevada railroad, and the little car, brave in the yellow paint and green trim that was to be the hallmark of the V. & T. from that day to this, was a thing of pride and joy along the line. Today, the oldest of the railroad's rolling stock, it reposes tranquilly in the Carson City yards where first it saw the light of day, taking its ease with dignity, full of years and honors and memories of the valiant days and roaring nights of Nevada's spendthrift youth.

The gas-illuminated ticket office lantern adorns the platform of the passenger depot and general offices of the Virginia & Truckee at Carson City. Handily adjacent, too, is a large bronze bell which is tolled to announce the departure of trains from this most venerable and shady of stations.

C. M. Clegg

CROSSROADS OF RAILROAD EMPIRE

Having set out its oil cars, to be picked up by a later Texas and Pacific way freight, and hooked onto a string of empty tanks for the fields around Breckenridge, the Wichita Falls & Southern's No. 30 rolls north over its crossover with the busy T. & P. main line at Ranger, Texas. Signals closing the T. & P. block are set by hand by the W. F. & S. head brakeman and released after his train has cleared the right-of-way.

THE CORNWALL'S ENGINES ARE NEVER TURNED

Item for a scrapbook is the Cornwall Railroad, deep in the green hills of Pennsylvania. Running between the large steel and iron foundries of Lebanon and the two-century-old mines of Cornwall, it abandoned passenger service in 1929, but its eight consolidations and 0-8-0 switchers daily haul from four to ten ore trains over the six miles of main line. The proprietors of the independently owned and operated Cornwall are fond of saying it is not as long as the connecting Pennsylvania, but just as wide. The ancient mines, furnaces, and forges of eighteenth-century Cornwall are legendary in Pennsylvania and might well have served for the prototype of the family property in Joseph Hergesheimer's famous story, "The Three Black Pennys." The railroad never turns its engines, which run forward to the mines and haul their load backward when they return.

C. M. Clegg

Lucius Beebe

FREIGHTED WITH MEMORIES FROM GOLDFIELD

In the brave days of 1905 and 1906 when the bonanza of Goldfield was at its fullest flower and the gold fever surged in a wave of hysteria through Nevada, three Pullman trains a day rolled into the desert diggings of Tonopah and Goldfield and the Tonopah and Goldfield Railroad shipped millions in precious ore by way of the Southern Pacific to the smelters and counting houses of San Francisco. Until recently Goldfield was a ghost town and Tonopah was concerned for the mining of a modest quantity of less precious metals and minerals. The big hotel at Goldfield was a haunted house, no longer did the glittering roulette wheels spin in the Bank Club and the Double Eagle; the Palace and Hermitage saloons were a memory and lizards sunned themselves among the cellarage debris of what had once been the glittering Montezuma Club. But the Tonopah and Goldfield still maintained a link, not only a geographic junction with the Southern Pacific at the base of the Monte Cristo Mountains, but a less tangible bond with the wonderful past. The ponderous gray fieldstone banks of Goldfield might close their doors and the false front Arcade Music Hall and Tex Richard's Northern might sell their last glass of forty rod, but the ancient Consolidations of the T. & G. still rolled their way across the bitter Nevada desert with oil and building materials and foodstuff, indeed all the necessities of life, for Tonopah. With the overnight San Francisco Pullman in its consist, a tandem of 2-8-0s is shown here at the smoky end of a mixed train under a July sun near Tonopah Junction. The recent easing of wartime restrictions on gold mining may mean renewed activity along the legendary Tonopah and Goldfield.

PRIDE AND POLISH IN DEEPEST TEXAS

Consolidation Type, No. 5, of the Weatherford, Mineral Wells & Northwestern, a feeder of the Texas and Pacific, rounds a curve in the well-manicured right-of-way at Garner, Texas.

C. M. Clegg

"SHE WENT BY DALE, AND SHE WENT BY DOWN"

"Lady Clare"

No more romantically bucolic railroad runs in steam than the Bellefonte Central down the rich mountain valleys of central Pennsylvania. Something of the informality of its trackage and right-of-way is indicated in this action picture taken at Briarly, Pennsylvania.

Lucius Beebe

WORKING STEAM ON THE SLIM-GAGE GRADE

The conventional tonnage for this sturdy narrow-gage Mike, No. 18, on the East Broad Top is twenty to twenty-five hoppers of coal from the mines whence it derives its name, with a passenger coach on scheduled runs. Mostly it takes the moderate grades in its stride, but here it is shown working steam and panting mightily on the long tangent leading to the yards at Mount Union.

Roger W. Grant, Courtesy of Trains

BELFAST AND MOOSEHEAD LAKE MIXED CONSIST

Over the tracks of the Maine Central at Burnham Junction rolls the polished ten-wheeler of the Belfast & Moosehead Lake with a mixed train ending in one of the road's six passenger coaches.

THE CAR THAT DOES EVERYTHING

This gas-electric railcar of the combined railways, the Kansas, Oklahoma & Gulf, the Oklahoma City-Ada-Atoka, and the Midland Valley, shown in the depot at Denison, Texas, serves the surrounding countryside in a variety of capacities: as railway post office and mail car, Railway Express Agency, and passenger transport. On runs where traffic is light such cars represent a considerable saving of fuel and crew service over conventional steam trains.

AT THE HAUNTED WATER TOWER

An oil burner, No. 30 of the Wichita Falls & Southern, pauses for refreshment at this slightly haunted-looking water tower along the road's overgrown right-of-way at Ranger, Texas.

Snorting, rolling, and rocking over the precarious roadbed under a brave cloud of oil smoke, the little train recedes over the uplands, past the ruined porch of the farmhouse which once served as McLennan depot and down the long grade into Ranger. At Ranger No. 44 sets out four cars of oil for the T. & P., picks up six empties and two carloads of feed for Breckenridge and a valuable flatload of oil pipes and rigging for north Texas, and the crew of four ties down the train and goes across the station square to Mrs. Higdon's Cafe. At Mrs. Higdon's the crew runs into the local agent of the Sinclair Refining Company's Pipeline Department, whose pipe they are taking north with them, and safe delivery at Wichita Falls is promised over the pie à la mode.

After lunch No. 44 again wheezes into activity. The head shack runs ahead to close down the main line of the T. & P. for its passage, the clattering Consolidation is watered at an ancient tower that is almost certainly haunted, and early afternoon sees it headed out on the remaining 130 miles of its run which will, with luck, be completed by ten o'clock that night. This is a busy day's operations on the Wichita Falls & Southern.

A few miles from the course of the famed Brazos River in Palo Pinto County, high in the rocky fastness of the hills of Texas, lies the sprawling resort town of Mineral Wells. The word of its neighboring scenic beauties in bygone years attracted a considerable tourist trade, but today its most celebrated product is Crazy Springs Mineral Water, a beverage of advertised tonic qualities consumed in impressive quantities at its numerous spas and pavilions and of which more than a million gallons a year are bottled and exported for off-premises consumption.

Although in recent times the tourist trade has diminished to a point where a stage line suffices for its accommodation, there exists to ferry out Crazy Water and the farm products cultivated in the nearby Lake Pinto dairy region one of the most elegant little railroads still in profitable operation in North America. Affiliated with the powerful Texas and Pacific and sharing its main-line trackage at its eastern terminus with the parent company, the Weatherford, Mineral Wells & Northwestern operates two mixed trains daily over a manicured right-of-way characterized by heavy rail, rock ballast, and scenic backgrounds.

Its motive power, designed along characteristic Texas and Pacific lines, sparkles from pilot beam to the markers on its tenders, and though its cabooses are initialed T. & P. crummies, its engines bear their own proud herald. The right-of-way through pleasant farmlands and rolling uplands covers thirty miles from its prosperous depot at Mineral Wells to its own private station a thousand yards down the line from the T. & P. platform at Weatherford, and the smoke of its sleek oil-burning Consolidations rolls wonderfully heavenward as Nos. 3 and 4 breast the two per cent grades at Wolters and Garner.

Generally speaking, neither the East nor the West has any monopoly on little railroads, but Pennsylvania is one of the most fruitful vicinages for the flowering of short lines, stub switches, venerable motive power, and the atmosphere of yesterday's high iron. Within fifty miles of each other there still flourish, as this is written, three short lines in the center of the Keystone Commonwealth which, although inaccessible in varying degrees, are choice items in the lexicon of the railroad historian and highlights in any pilgrimage of amateurs of pure Americana.

One of the merest handful of narrow-gage railroads scattered between California and the Atlantic seaboard, the East Broad Top Railroad & Coal Company, whose parent corporation is the Rockhill Coal and Iron Company, shares, roughly speaking, the resources of the East Broad Top coal fields with the adjacent and almost parallel Huntingdon and Broad Top Mountain Railroad a few miles to the west. The East Broad Top taps the deposits on the east side of the mountain range, the Huntingdon and Broad Top Mountain those on its western slope, and both feed freight and passenger service into the Middle Division of the Pennsylvania Railroad at Mount Union and Huntingdon, respectively, which are eleven miles apart. The East Broad Top is three-foot-gaged, the Huntingdon and Broad Top Mountain standard, and each of them is a collector's item of the first magnitude among amateurs of smalltime railroading.

Probably the only parallel, so far as maintenance and style of railroading is concerned in the field of narrow gage, to the three-foot divisions of the Denver and Rio Grande Western, the East Broad Top is very much of a going concern and its motive power, heavy rails, and sub-

Lucius Beebe

THE MINERS' TRAIN

At the close of the working day the narrow-gage East Broad Top Railroad & Coal Company runs this two-coach train with a caboose from the Broad Top ridges and strip coal mines back to Orbisonia, stopping from time to time to let the miners off at their homes along the way. Something of the backwoods spirit of American railroading is captured as the little train passes through a clearing in the woods at Saltillo, Pennsylvania.

stantial ballast would do credit to many a road operating over more conventionally spaced iron. It was built in 1873, in a generation when narrow-gage construction was in almost universal vogue, and all its clearances are such that it is able to handle foreign cars from other railroads by the simple expedient of shifting them to narrow-gage trucks by means of a hoist located in its Mount Union yards.

Except for two coach trains run for miners over its main line daily, the East Broad Top's scheduled trains serving Shirleysburg, Orbisonia, and a variety of smaller way-stations, are of mixed consist, carrying one or two incredibly ancient coaches at the end of a string of twenty or twenty-five coal hoppers. The coaches for many years were familiar sights running across the Boston salt meadows on the communting trains of the now vanished Boston, Revere Beach, and Lynn.

Although the corporate articles of the East Broad Top nominate it as a coal company, its activities are in the field of transportation only. Its approximately fifty miles of operating track serve a very sparsely populated geographic locale and its sole warrant for existence lies in the mining activities it exploits and whose existence, in turn, it jealously guards. When the mines are seasonally closed its mail, light freight, and passengers are transported by gas-electric car, but when business is good six narrow-gage Mikes, one Prairie, and two standard-gage switchers operating on the Pennsylvania transfer tracks all roll together in the last surviving slim-gage run of consequence in the East.

The operations of the Huntingdon and Broad Top Mountain Railroad in many ways beside that of territory served, parallel those of the neighboring narrow-gage road. It is primarily a coal-haul road; it has direct connection with the main line of the Pennsylvania's Middle division; it is an old and established organization dating from the time when the Pennsy was more numerously fed by branch railroads some of which— the Tuscarora Valley, the Newport and Sherman's Valley, and the southwestern trackage of the Bellefonte Central—no longer operate. Differing from the East Broad Top, the H. & B. T. M. is of conventional gage, has more extensive passenger traffic, and is faced with more considerable problems in getting the coal out of the strip mines on the three branches of its own trackage to Garlick Mine, Finleyville, Broad Top.

To overcome the last of these it employs an elaborate system of switchbacks and at one point an aerial tramway. Its passenger hauls of which there are several on daily schedule for varying distances on its main line are handled by a specially assigned passenger locomotive, No. 30, a handsome American Type 4-4-0 with high drivers and a capped stack which has been running on the H. & B. T. M. since 1907. The H. & B. T. M. carries its passengers in something resembling style and runs a blue-painted, modern steel coach for this purpose as well as a matching mail-and-goods car. At Huntingdon the little road has its own track into the platform of the Pennsylvania depot. Years ago when the H. & B. T. M. first operated, both its track and the four main-line rails of the Pennsy ran on the other side of the low brick station building and a canal occupied their present site. Today the canal exists only in the memories of old-timers in the neighborhood and the cars and engine of the H. & B. T. M., when they are at their terminal, are visible to passengers who are minded to look out of the windows of the Broadway, General, or Spirit of St. Louis as they thunder through Huntingdon without slowing.

To say that the Bellefonte Central Railroad is a phantom line running between nowhere and nowhere would, geographically speaking, be in error and would also be the occasion of grief to residents in several agreeable communities in the fantastically lovely hill country of mid-Pennsylvania. But socially, economically, and industrially, it would be essentially true. As persons are classified in their police dossiers as being "without visible means of support," so is the Bellefonte Central, for, while its northern terminus, Bellefonte, actually connects with the all-powerful Pennsylvania, and its southern is the shaded and leisured academe of State College, some eighteen miles distant, between the two there are scant apparent means to support its operations. There is a daily train, mixed, each way, through the townships of Pleasant Gap, Hunters Park, Briarly, Houseville, and Krumrine, not to mention Waddle and Fillmore. Its tracks, often unfenced, run through meadows and pastures with brooks which attract the Brown Hackles and Silver Doctors of fly fishermen. Willow trees arch theatrically across the right-of-way, geese parade down its ballast, and traffic is almost daily impeded by placid cows. It is the sort of railroad that must have run through rural Pennsylvania a full century ago, when all the world was young and the train brigade a new and perilous enterprise. A reading of the Georgic verses of James Thomson's "The Seasons" would not have been dismayed or disturbed by the passing of its daily mixed consist. Had Watteau painted in its time, the Bellefonte Central would have been Watteau's railroad. The Bellefonte Central is a fine thing to see, a gentle and heartening railroad to know.

These are but traces of a few little railroads, arbitrarily selected from within the experience and knowledge of the author. There are many scores of others and their stories and outlines alone may, happily, one day be collected by some pious chronicler in a volume entirely dedicated to the high iron that is grass grown and the rights-of-way that wander amiably under tall trees and in forgotten places. Rust on the rails may often be a patina of the most compelling charm.

Lucius Beebe

C. M. Clegg

2
Power for the Grade

WAR IS not necessarily an unmitigated abomination to the railroads most directly affected by it. To be sure, if a railroad lies in the region of combat action, an area whose diameter has been enormously increased by modern destructive technique, it is one of the first objects of hostile attention as was the case of the railroads of the Confederacy during the Civil War and, more recently, the railroads of England and the European continent. Nor is a railroad system that is removed a tolerable distance from factual military activity like that of the United States in both World Wars I and II, immune from a variety of confusion, dismay, and disarrangements of its normal function; but in return for these several circumstances of harassment it may very well stand to benefit from a number of directions.

Through the agency of direct government control the railroads of the United States emerged from the first World War in a state of almost complete dislocation and impoverishment of their resources. It is probable that they will survive the second World War in better condition than they were before the date of Pearl Harbor.

There have, of course, been headaches, many of them of museum-piece proportions: loss of personnel to the military, the need for wartime conversion with unaccustomed urgency, the abatement of time-honored operations traditions, and the loss of passenger prestige among travelers whose patronage has been forever alienated by the arbitrary whims of an Office of Defense Transportation and the coöperative neglect of railroad managements themselves. There is both irony and tragedy in the approach of the inevitable day when railroads will have to attempt to recapture the favor of passengers whose patronage they discouraged with advertising and abused with discourtesy and inconvenience under the gaudy but frequently spurious excuse of military necessity. Nor have railroads been able to wring from the Federal government a fraction of the matériel which would have made their over-all task less of a miracle in its accomplishment.

Offsetting these deficits, however, there have been boons and usufructs of indisputable and enduring proportions. Fixed charges and corporate indebtedness have been substantially reduced, in some cases as much as 65 per cent. Vast outstanding obligations have been liquidated, bonds called, interest charges lowered, and a general fiscal tidying-up accomplished.

New economies of operation, too, have been evolved on every hand and in many cases great improvements have been made in the actual physical assets of important railroads. Generally speaking, maintenance of roadbeds and installations have kept ahead of maintenance and replacement of motive power and rolling stock. Light rails have been replaced by heavier steel, curves and grades eliminated, bridges, viaducts and improved trackage facilities built, Centralized Traffic Control instituted, and signal and communications systems improved. While standards of passenger transport have visibly declined, tremendous increases in freight tonnage have been expedited at impressively stepped-up speeds and the position of the railroads as postwar carriers of all classifications of goods tremendously strengthened.

War has brought about a tremendous shrinkage of the railroad companies' corporate waistlines and a beneficial hardening of their operative sinews. While it is difficult to force from any railroad executive an admission that his line is enjoying bonanza times, very few carriers can be said to be operating in borrasca. And many and many a little railroad and short line has been living happily and even sumptuously on, on borrowed time!

Specifically, the most tangible aspect of wartime progress, so far as the public imagination is concerned, has been the expansion of Diesel-electric motive power, not in the passenger field for which it was originally designed, but as a freight mover. Other innovations have been evolved by the score: the construction of immense classification yards under central control such as has been characteristic of Burlington expansion; the building of magnificent bridges and short cuts such as those of the Santa Fe over the Colorado at Topock and the Rock Island's crossing of the Cimmaron in southwestern Kansas; the building of the first aluminum box cars for the Alton and the Minneapolis & St. Louis, and the instalation of C.T.C. on scores of roads ranging from the Cotton Belt to the Kansas City Southern, the Seaboard Air Line, the Southern Pacific, and the Denver & Rio Grande Western. But the most spectacular advance has been the appearance of Diesel jacks on scores of freight runs where hotshots and drags alike have for decades and generations been powered by the steam-expansion locomotive of established tradition.

No comprehensive survey of wartime expansion of Diesel-electric power would be practicable in the space available here nor would it long remain a valid record in changing times, but there are aspects which are not without their interest even to the sentimental and practical steam-power supporter.

Six years after the first successful use of Diesel-electric power in passenger service, the Electro-Motive Division of General Motors, in 1940, introduced the first Diesel freight unit. In January, 1941, the Santa Fe placed in operating service the first 5400-horsepower freight engine on its roster, and by mid-1945 more than 1300 Diesel freight units of varying tonnage capacities were in service, more than five times as many as were running on passenger hauls. Three competing firms were building Diesel freight locomotives and there was being heard talk of complete Dieselization of divisions and even whole railroad systems.

From the world's first Diesel freight operation inaugurated in 1941, the Santa Fe's Diesel freight fleet has grown to sixty-nine 5400-horsepower locomotives, practically all of which are in service in one of the world's most spectacular operations, the 459 miles between Winslow, Arizona, and Barstow, California. Here is one of the toughest pieces of railroad, from the standpoint of operating conditions, in the United States. The problem was complicated through the war period by the volume of freight which frequently reached the point where no more trains could be put on the double-tracked district and maintain the fast schedules required. There were days when trains operated through a given point in the district as often as every fifteen minutes. Local water conditions are bad. Before Diesel operation it was necessary to transport three million gallons of water a day to one point. The profile ranges from 400 feet above sea level at Needles, California, to 7,355 feet

Courtesy of the Chicago, Burlington & Quincy

ROLLING THE TANKS THROUGH WYOMING

This striking view of the Chicago, Burlington & Quincy's new 5400-horsepower Diesel-electric freight units was taken as it rolled a string of 100 oil tanks north through Sheep Canyon, Wyoming, en route from Texas to the Pacific Northwest on the road's Denver-Caspar-Billings line. Over the routes of the famous Fort Worth and Denver City and the Colorado and Southern, now integral units of the Burlington system, the C. B. & Q. can haul oil from the port of Galveston, Texas, on the Gulf of Mexico, all the way to Billings, Montana, almost to the Canadian border, without leaving its own iron, of which it owns or controls 11,000 miles in thirteen states with direct contact or direct connections with every important community west of the Mississippi River.

ST. LOUIS-SAN FRANCISCO SUPERPOWER ON PARADE

Breasting the mile-long grade out of Valley Park, Missouri, a few miles west of St. Louis on the Frisco's main line, one of the tremendous 4-8-4s of the 4500 Class heads into a rising sun with nearly 100 cars of redball freight behind it. A quarter of a mile away are visible the cars of a Missouri Pacific drag on the west line for Kansas City dropping down the same grade.

Lucius Beebe

"WHILE SMOKE BLACK FREIGHTS ON THE DOUBLE
TRACKED RAILROAD
DRIVEN AS THOUGH BY THE FOUL FIEND'S OX-GOAD..."

Vachel Lindsay

A gleaming Chesapeake and Ohio light Mallet picks up speed on the down grade
out of Manassas, Virginia, with a string of empty coal cars three-quarters of a
mile long bound for the coal fields of Kentucky and West Virginia on the end-
less shuttle between the mine tipples and the seaports and manufacturing citadels
of the industrial East.

Lucius Beebe

WHITE FLAGS WESTWARD

A Chicago and North Western Mikado running extra ahead of a long drag of wartime freight consigned to the Pacific coast rolls its tonnage ponderously over the long hill on the east approach to Geneva, Illinois. Notice the left-hand operations, typical of all the trackage of the road, which was financed by British capital and which has ever since its inception retained this characteristic English convention of traffic.

THREESOME ON THE MILWAUKEE ROAD

Above is a Chicago, Milwaukee, St. Paul & Pacific time freight with a heavy-duty Mikado on the smoky end near Watertown, Wisconsin, on the Milwaukee-Portage run.

At the top of the page opposite is the Afternoon Hiawatha powered by a twin Diesel-electric unit hitting eighty-five just south of Milwaukee on the Chicago–Twin Cities run, while below it is the Chippeawa, streamlined in steam on the daily noontime run between Chicago, Milwaukee, Green Bay, Iron Mountain and Ontonagon.

IN IOWA, WHERE THE TALL CORN GROWS

This serene countryside could hardly be anywhere but in the opulent and comfortably nourished state of Iowa where fat dairies and broad cornlands reach as far as the eye can see. Through this lush pastoral the Burlington's Class 05, No. 5601, rolls through a summer evening ahead of seventy-five cars of time freight No. 61 two miles west of Red Oak.

THIS ENGINE SHOWS ITS INNARDS

Advocates of streamlining and simplification of engine design doubtless recoil from the practice which hangs a locomotive's pumps on the front of its smokebox and shamelessly exposes its pipes and feedlines, but a more robust school of railroad amateurs will admire the Chesapeake and Ohio's train No. 5, the Sportsman, westbound as it breasts the long graded tangent leading to Manassas, Virginia, with silver paint on the driver tires and stars on the cylinder heads of Mountain Type No. 544.

THE C. & E. I. DIXIE LIMITED

The heavy Pacifics of the Chicago & Eastern Illinois have a style and carriage as is shown by this no longer young engine picking its way through the yards at Forty-seventh Street, Chicago, on the smoky end of the Dixie Limited. Note the dropped headlight, bell hung between the domes, straight boiler and perforated sheet steel pilot.

BACK FROM THE BONEYARD

Believe it or not, this tandem of period-design engines, whose thundering contrapuntal blasts shake the California heavens, are heading a main-line fast freight on the Southern Pacific's iron a few miles south of San Jose on the Coast Route to Los Angeles. A few years before, these vintage Consolidations may have been serving as yard goats in Salinas or Bakersfield, but the war brought ghosts back to the Espee's manifest runs, and the high-domed ancients are rolling down among the orange groves with a mile of mixed freight behind them and youthful fireboys keeping the pressure gages jerking. Tumultuous and smoky, these 2-8-os are reliving their flaming youth. Never again, in all probability, will there be such a parade across the mountains and meadows of the land as was occasioned by the wars, and locomotives which had passed the half-century mark were, on scores of lines, retrieved from yard duties and forgotten roundhouses and once again conditioned for main-line operations. The axiom that a locomotive never really wears out was demonstrated when American type 4-4-os of the Cotton Belt reappeared in the St. Louis terminal and when forty-year-old 2-8-os of the Southern rolled into the Potomac Yards at Alexandria with long trains of stock cars and fruit blocks from Florida; and the hearts of old-timers were stirred by high-wheel Atlantics once again breasting the iron from the Illinois cornfields to the prairies of Texas.

TIDY LITTLE FRISCO MIKE

Unlike the farther north divisions of the St. Louis–San Francisco where the operational technique calls for far heavier tonnage behind the drawbars of impressive motive power, the custom in Texas is to dispatch light trains of twenty or twenty-five cars behind lighter engines. There is no concentration of traffic to require the handling of a maximum possible load in each train operation. Here, a mile below the Texas–Oklahoma boundary near Denison, a Frisco Mikado, with a tender cab and flying white, wheels a short cut of cars across the countryside with a great deal of railroading style.

Lucius Beebe

TIME FREIGHT ON THE WABASH

To "Wabash" was once in railroad jargon a verb meaning to handle a locomotive with unusual dexterity and speed, and a handy engine driver was known as a "Wabash artist." This powerful Northern Type engine at the head of seventy-five cars of redball freight at Granite City, Illinois, northbound, is carrying on the road's tradition of competent operations and speedy traffic.

Lucius Beebe

AMONG THE VIRGINIA RAIL FENCES

The first Consolidation type locomotive was built by Baldwin for the Lehigh Valley Railroad in 1866 and its use has been universal and constant from that day to this. Today it is becoming increasingly rare, but still can be found in service on light hauls. This example of its class is stepping along at a lively forty miles an hour with thirty-odd stock cars on the Southern's branch line near Front Royal Junction, Virginia, en route to Manassas and, eventually, the classification yards at Alexandria. Notice the square steam-chests, characteristic of engine design forty years ago, and the bell fixed to the top of the smoke-box. It was this branch of the Southern's trackage, joining the main line at Manassas, which in civil war times caused the town on whose outskirts the battles of Bull Run were fought to be known as Manassas Junction. Between Washington and Charlottesville, Virginia, the Chesapeake and Ohio and the Southern share the same rails for both freight and passenger service.

R. F. Collins, Courtesy of Railroad Magazine

ERIE TIME FREIGHT MAKING TIME

Erie fast freight No. 91 near Susquehanna, Pennsylvania, running at sixty behind Mikado No. 4201.

C. M. Clegg

PASTORAL AND PURPOSEFUL. LEHIGH VALLEY
COAL DRAG

PRESIDENTIAL ECONOMY

In leaner years when the Katy was shaving expenses, President Matthew Sloan forewent the accustomed special trains and business cars which attach to ranking executive office and made inspection trips in an M-K-T automobile fitted with flanges and a self-contained turntable, and painted a Katy yellow with a pilot, special lamps, and horns. Stockholders appreciated the economy and division and track superintendents had duplicates run up for their official inspection tours.

C. M. Clegg

THE NEWEST THING IN CLASSIFICATION YARDS

Designed to speed the classification of freight impinging upon Lincoln, Nebraska, from the four points of the compass over the main lines of the Chicago, Burlington & Quincy, this freight hump with its electro-pneumatic car retarders and 265 switches operated from control towers will save in excess of 175,000 car days each year. Lincoln is the hub of the Burlington lines west of the Missouri River with its principal spokes radiating to Denver and California, to Billings and the Pacific Northwest, to Chicago on the east and to Kansas City, Sioux City and St. Louis. The yards comprise sixty-five miles of track, which is more than the entire mileage of a good many railroads of more modest rank.

ELEPHANT EARS IN VERMONT

Smoke deflectors of innumerable types have been the subject of experiments on almost every American railroad. Faired-in sidewall steel plates of the type shown here on Central Vermont light Pacific No. 230 helping B. & M. Pacific No. 3628 at Westminster, Vermont, are an importation from abroad where they have for many years been standard on English and continental railroads. Other roads which have experimented more or less successfully with such "elephant-ears" are the New York Central, Nickel Plate, Canadian National, Boston and Maine, Delaware and Hudson, and Pennsylvania.

THE OVERLAND MAIL

From Reno, Nevada, to Ogden, Utah, over the route of the legendary Central Pacific is 533 miles by the iron of the Southern Pacific and one of the most desolate of all North American main-line runs. Only Carlin, Elko, Winnemucca, and a handful of slimly populated mining communities are along the way, slowly disintegrating souvenirs of once rich mining days and the gaudy saga of the authentically wild west. Here in a lonely mountain canyon between Sparks and Fernley a few miles east of the end of double-track operations an Espee Santa Fe type engine, carrying green for a following section and trailing a rolling cloud of oil smoke, charges eastward with fifteen cars of the mails over the single track which is the principal life-line between Chicago and San Francisco. There are only two other railroad routes operating between the Golden Gate and the cities of the Middle West: the Feather River line of the Western Pacific Railroad through the Sierras a few miles to the north, and the Southern Pacific's own division, shared by the Santa Fe, far to the south by way of Bakersfield and Fresno. With the exception of the City of San Francisco no Espee trains are carded on such a fast schedule between East and West as the government's mails. The photograph was taken with a Speed Graphic at 1/300 second on Kodak Super XX film with a lens opening of 6.5 f.

C. M. Clegg

CATCHALL IN NEW JERSEY

Near Suffern, New Jersey, an Erie light Pacific with its characteristic Vanderbilt type tender, hauls the mails, baggage, and local freight, pausing at every station to set down or pick up its wares while the Erie Limited and Midlander thunder around it.

Below left: Not many miles away Donald Furler has captured the spirit of a Reading time freight working steam near Bound Brook.

Lucius Beebe

THE MEET

At Sullivan, Missouri, the Frisco's Northern Type No. 4503, a powerful 4-8-4 flying green with seventy cars of redball freight attached to its drawbar has gone into the passing track and is being held by a red board. Emerging from the yards on the main after pausing at the coal tipple shown in the background are Mountain Type No. 1508 running as helper ahead of road engine No. 4414 with a long drag of coal headed into St. Louis. As soon as the eastbound drag clears the switch, No. 4503 will continue on its way.

C. M. Clegg

SILVER AND PURPLE OF THE A.C.L.

Running late with twenty cars of Pullman and coach passengers, and head-end revenue freight, the Atlantic Coast Line's Champion, West Coast Section, rumbles northward a few miles north of Richmond, Virginia, over the right-of-way of the Richmond, Fredericksburg & Potomac Railroad.

IN THE CORNLANDS OF THE MIDDLE WEST

The great bulk of the right-of-way of the Illinois Central runs south of Chicago toward New Orleans, adjacent to the Mississippi and bisecting the continent from Lake Michigan to the Gulf of Mexico, but a single east-west division stretches at right angles from this pattern and parallels the Chicago and North Western from Chicago to Omaha. It taps the rich agriculture of Nebraska, Iowa, and Illinois, and here is an eastbound extra behind Mikado No. 1429 highballing through Genoa, Illinois, with a long train of high cars and reefers filled with farm produce headed for Chicago and the markets of the East.

H. W. Pontin, Courtesy of Railroad Photographs

SOMETHING NEW IN OLD NEW ENGLAND

A Boston and Maine oil special eastbound from Mechanicville to Boston on the Fitchburg Division at Stony Brook, Massachusetts, is powered by the latest thing in Diesel-electric motive power on this historic Down East railroad.

A LEG-UP FOR EL CAPITAN

Upper left:
H. Sullivan

Amidst the wild and gloomy rock formations of the San Bernardino Mountains of California, one of the Santa Fe's light Pacifics of venerable vintage assists the streamlined Diesel-electric all-coach, extra-fare El Capitan up to 2.2 per cent grade of the east approach to the Cajon Pass. El Capitan runs between Los Angeles and Chicago twice a week each way on Super Chief schedule and is the only extra-fare coach train in the country.

THE SNORE AND GRUMBLE OF THE DIESEL

Lower left:
C. M. Clegg

Five or six miles east of Bull Run at Manassas Junction, Virginia, where railroading played its first important part in modern warfare, the muffled throb of a Southern Diesel-electric freight unit echoes across the winter fields with a mile of varied consist, mostly empties from the Potomac Yards south of Washington. It is a far cry from the balloon stacks of the brightly painted eight-wheelers which, in the first years of the Sixties, carried supplies for the Union troops before their dismaying defeat in the opening battle of the War of the States.

at Riordan, Arizona. Grades of varying severity to as high as 1.8 per cent are almost incessant.

The Santa Fe Dieselized all through freight operation between Winslow and Barstow and handled the load. One key to how the Santa Fe managed to keep the line clear under its back-breaking traffic lies in the fact that the load limit for the largest Santa Fe type steam locomotive in operation before Dieselization was 2000 tons. The limit for the Diesels was immediately raised to 3500 tons—the difference between fifty- and eighty- or ninety-car trains.

Smaller, but spectacular from the standpoint of results, was the Dieselization of through freight on the Erie between Marion, Ohio, and Meadville, Pennsylvania. Prior to the application of six 5400-horsepower Diesels to this district late in 1944 it was necessary to break the 100- to 125-car trains from the Middle West bound for Jersey City into two and sometimes three trains at Marion in order to enable the former motive power to make the time and keep yards clear. Similar procedure was followed at Meadville on westbound trains. After the six Diesels were put on the district, all through trains proceeded in both directions without breaking.

Diesel crews have taken some jibes in the past over the fact that steam helpers boost the western transcontinental streamlined trains over the worst climbs. The Diesel boys turned the joke when the Great Northern installed one 4500-horsepower Diesel freighter on Walton Hill, near Glacier Park. The one locomotive—which is only three-fourths of the most powerful Diesel model—replaced three Mallets in this helper service on the twenty-five-mile grade. Two Mallets were on duty and one was kept in reserve. One of the Mallets was kept at Walton Hill for emergencies for several months after the Diesel arrived. No emergencies arose so the Mallet was sent where it could do some work.

The Boston and Maine uses its fleet of twelve 5400-horsepower Diesels in main-line freight service between Boston and Mechanicville, New York, a run of 189 miles, ordinarily non-stop. The run with 125-car trains is completed ordinarily in six and a half hours, against former time of ten to fourteen hours.

The Chicago, Milwaukee, St. Paul & Pacific railroad put four 5400-

horsepower Diesels in service between Othello, Washington, and Avery, Idaho, connecting its two electrified zones. This had been a bottleneck in the movement of wartime freight, since breaking of trains after they left the electrified zones was necessary. It was found that the four Diesels took the trains without breaking through the heavily mountainous, un-electrified district of 226 miles and cut the time in half. In short, what the Milwaukee got was electrified results without the cost of electrification.

Use of the electric transmission in the Diesel locomotive gave the designers opportunity to add a piece of equipment which, in some operations, has meant almost as much in speeding up movement of freight as has the inherent advantage of the propulsion machinery. This equipment is the electric retarding brake, familiar to those who have studied electric locomotive operation in the Rockies. The Diesel designers have gone one step further in the development of this brake, making it applicable at any speed and capable of holding the train at any desired speed, within certain limits of effectiveness controlled by extreme grades. The earlier electric retarding brakes on electric locomotives hold the train at certain speeds.

The principle of the electric retarding brake, sometimes called the dynamic brake, is simple. Turning of a switch lever by the engineer reverses the wiring of the traction motors and makes them generators. Generators resist motion. In fact, in the 5400-horsepower GM locomotive these brakes will exert a maximum of 4300-horsepower in braking effect. This is sufficient to hold a heavy train to safe speeds on all but the steepest grades without the use of air brakes. As persons familiar with railroad operation know, one of the limiting factors in the schedules of freight trains is time required to get down grades. There are divisions where trains with conventional brakes can get up a given grade faster they can get down the same grade. This is due to the fact that when air brakes are used heavily for long periods both the brake shoes and wheels get heated past the safety point, and it often is necessary to stop freights both in the middle and at the bottom of the grade for as long as an hour to permit shoes and wheels to cool, and to make the necessary inspection of wheels and shoes after the overheating. Frequently brake shoes have to be replaced. The electric retarding brake has eliminated this source of lost time and expense. The application of air brakes to assist the retarding brake is so light and for such short periods that wheels and shoes do not overheat.

After this feature had proven itself thoroughly in mountainous country the Burlington Lines put sixteen 5400's into service in the prairie country between Chicago and Denver. To the astonishment of some they ordered the locomotives equipped with the electric retarding brake. The Burlington then proceeded to demonstrate the usefulness of the brake in level operation. It was found that frequently a heavy freight with a clear track could operate as much as 150 miles without a single application of air. The retarding brakes were sufficient to handle all slow orders. The saving in wheels and shoes has been considerable. The Burlington also reports that the brake has helped cut time because the locomotive can accelerate immediately after the brakes are released, whereas if train brakes have been applied sharply for a curve or other slow condition, it is necessary to drift until sufficient time has elapsed to allow brakes to release the full length of the train.

Veteran hoggers who have become masters in the difficult art of trundling long heavy drags smoothly over rolling, curved profiles say that the retarding brakes practically add a new dimension to train handling. They soon learn how to use the retarding brake in combination with throttle and train and independent air brakes, and the results they achieve are best described as artistic. Laymen who have seen some of these men operate grope for the right description and usually end by comparing the engineer with an accomplished pipe-organ player.

That the emergence of Diesel-electric power, like the consolidation of the great railway systems of the land, was an unmitigated calamity so far as the romantic and picturesque aspects of the railroad legend is concerned, is undeniable. Even the reappearance of color in trains made possible by the absence of soot is insufficient compensation for the enchantments of steam and smoke, outside motion, and the atmosphere of hurrah which once were part of yesterday's railroading.

Just what of homely charm or vigor passengers will find to kindle the imagining in the railroad of tomorrow, the pattern and shape of which are beginning to emerge in the institutional advertising copy of car builders, locomotive foundries, the roads themselves, and their most notable confraternity, the Association of American Railroads, is difficult to envision. That rail travel will be vastly expedited, rendered increasingly luxurious and, if possible in the light of already existing standards, safer, may be regarded as an accomplished fact.

It may turn out, however, that the golden age of American railroading was in its florid, imperial years, the age of the bonanza railways of the Far West, of looped and fringed curtains in Silver Palace cars, conductors in mutton chop whiskers and blue tailcoats, of the sparks exploding from the tall stacks of Taunton-built high wheelers with crimson and gold lettering on their tenders, and of highball signals on hand-operated halyards before the first decadence of semaphores and traces of decline inherent in the air brake.

Lucius Beebe

C. M. Clegg

3

PORTRAIT GALLERY

C. M. Clegg

OLD RELIABLE DOBBIN OF THE HIGH IRON

When it left Denver the day before, the Burlington's Texas Zephyr was a completely streamlined train powered by a sleek silver Diesel-electric unit. Between Colorado and Texas, however, things happened. The Diesel unit went into a decline and had to be detached at Fort Worth. Also two coaches and a Pullman of standard design were picked up en route. So here we see the Zephyr on the tracks between Fort Worth and Dallas shared with the Rock Island, six hours off schedule and rolling like a proverbial bat out of hell to make up some of its lost time behind a reliable, old-time steam Pacific.

Lucius Beebe

ALONG THE EAST SHORE OF THE HUDSON

Train No. 41, the Knickerbocker, bound for St. Louis and Cincinnati, pulls out of Harmon, New York, behind one of the Hudson locomotives which are the standard passenger power of the New York Central on its "water level route" between New York and the Middle West.

Lucius Beebe

NO. 26, THE MERCHANT'S EXPRESS

Every weekday morning at 7:15 the Delaware, Lackawanna and Western's Merchant's Express starts on its run of 135 miles from Scranton to New York, its individual seat coaches and diner-buffet crowded with brokers and commuting business men bound for the big city. Here it is shown rolling east under a cloud of coal smoke at the long viaduct on the Lackawanna Cutoff at Gainesville, New Jersey, three miles east of the Delaware Water Gap which separates New Jersey from the Commonwealth of Pennsylvania.

Lucius Beebe

THE SOUTHERN PACIFIC'S DAYLIGHT, OLD AND NEW

Southern Pacific

Richard J. Cook

THE RED BIRD ON THE WABASH

On the Chicago–St. Louis run the Wabash's most notable daylight varnish train is the afternoon Blue Bird. On the Chicago-Detroit daylight haul its crack flier is the Red Bird shown here rolling into Montpelier, Ohio, behind Pacific No. 689, with coaches, two parlor cars, and diner as well as an observation buffet car for coach passengers. A classic portrait of a classic passenger train in the old manner.

C. M. Clegg

PERFECTION IN LOCOMOTIVE POWER

At Denison, Texas, the Missouri-Kansas-Texas Train No. 1-11, the Texas Special, splits on its southern haul into two sections, one for Fort Worth, the other for the skyscraper metropolis of Dallas. With the Katy's famed shield in red and white ornamenting its tender and mail car, the Dallas section of the road's proudest varnish run rolls down an autumn sunrise near Whiteright, Texas, behind a high-wheel Pacific brave with white-trimmed footboards, to make a pluperfect photographic study of railroad action.

A MIKADO HAULS ITS TONNAGE

Just east of Gaithersburg on the Baltimore and Ohio's main line between Washington and Cumberland there is a gently rolling countryside of broad meadows, pastures, and cornfields. Here, against a georgic setting of autumn trees, a B. & O. Mikado whose driver has his reverse gear notched well forward on its quadrant, walks up a mile-long grade with a hundred cars of mixed consist. Freshly shopped and gleaming in the sun, No. 4419 is a fine study of this class of power so widely favored by the B. & O. The Mikado locomotive, or 2-8-2 type according to Whyte's classification, was evolved by Baldwin in 1897 in an order for motive power for the Japanese railways. In order to assure greater heating area in the firebox it was removed from the position it had until then occupied between the rearmost driving wheels and carried by a separate pair of diminutive trailing wheels. In time, as fireboxes increased in weight and dimensions, they came to be supported on four-wheel trucks and today some are borne on trailer carriages of six wheels.

Lucius Beebe

SUPERPOWER ON THE LEHIGH VALLEY

At Flemington Junction, New Jersey, a two-mile tangent on the main line of the Lehigh Valley furnished the opportunity for this action shot of one of the L. V.'s big 4-8-4s wheeling a time freight inbound toward the Jersey City yards.

THE INDIVIDUALISTIC JOHN WILKES

A study in modernistic design and bright coloring, the Lehigh Valley's John
Wilkes running from Coxton, Pennsylvania, to Jersey City and New York,
where it enters the Pennsylvania Station, is shown a mile north of Flemington
Junction, New Jersey.

C. M. Clegg

NIGHT SKY FOR A BACKGROUND

Running northbound into Denison, Texas, the Missouri-Kansas-Texas Blue-
bonnet bound for St. Louis nears the Oklahoma boundary with a trailing plume
of smoke exhaust unrolling against the Texas evening sky.

POLISH AND PERFECTION, NORTH FROM DIXIE

The Southern's No. 4852, a beautifully proportioned Mikado, noses up a grade among the yellow autumn cornfields of Virginia near Charlottesville with five cars of military personnel bound for a northern port of embarkation during the war year of 1944. The Southern's Mikes often serve in dual service roles as either freight or passenger engines when they are appropriate to the tonnage, much as Northerns and Mountain locomotives are used in dual service on western roads.

Lucius Beebe

TRIM BOSTON AND ALBANY PACIFIC

A local on the Boston-Worcester run shows its paces as it rolls through the Newtons a little west of Faneuil Station. A Pullman is riding deadhead ahead of the baggage car.

THE ALTON'S BEST FOOT FORWARD

Sometimes the Alton's Ann Rutledge on the Chicago–St. Louis daily run is powered with a Diesel-electric unit, but here it is shown on the speedway north of Granite City, Illinois, behind one of the road's well-kept heavy-duty Pacifics as it thunders down the right-of-way with its train of handsomely matched and colorfully varnished coaches, Pullmans, and lounge cars. The Alton's competition on this run is furnished by the Wabash, Chicago & Eastern Illinois, and Illinois Central.

Lucius Beebe

TANDEM TEAM FROM THE FRISCO STABLE

Near Valley Park, Missouri, a long coal drag with a team of iron horses, the helper a 4-8-2, the road engine a 4-8-4, pound up the grade toward St. Louis on the heavy iron of the Frisco.

SUNSHINE SPECIAL, NORTH TEXAS SECTION

Hitting its stride near Arlington Downs on the speedway between Fort Worth and Dallas, the Texas and Pacific's No. 2 behind a sightly 900 Class Mountain engine heads for the east and north on the run that will bring it into St. Louis the next morning. Manpower shortage or none, the T. & P.'s motive power has never been anything but magnificently cared for as is attested by No. 902's burnished cylinder heads, polished light-weight rod assembly, and generally sleek and prosperous appearance.

SUPERPOWER IN THE NEW JERSEY MEADOWS

Few railroads possess the variety of motive power which appears on the rosters of the Lehigh Valley, a Class 1 railroad with 1221 miles of track mostly between Buffalo and the harbor areas of Jersey City and Perth Amboy. The Pennsylvania Railroad, through the agency of the Wabash, owns a controlling interest in the Lehigh but doesn't interest itself in its operations. Its freight locomotives run from Consolidations and Mikados to 4-8-4's and Mountain Type 4-8-2's like the one shown here at the head end of a heavy drag climbing a slight grade on the mile-long tangent at Raritan, New Jersey. The Lehigh's passenger engines come in almost as many varieties of plain and fancy dress as the celebrated fifty-seven varieties of pickles, and several other examples of its power are visible elsewhere in this book.

Lucius Beebe

COTTON BELT CONSOLIDATION

At Addison, Texas, on the run from Commerce to Dallas with a short cut of mixed freight, a well-kept Cotton Belt Consolidation streaks for town under a rolling cloud of smoke exhaust. The combination foot-boards and conventional pilot indicate it is used in dual service both for yard duty and as a road engine.

Lucius Beebe

GREEN AND GOLD AND SMOKE ON THE SOUTHERN

Even in wartime the Southern contrived to keep its passenger motive power tolerably burnished and well-shopped. The tires, cylinder heads, and footboards of this green and gold Pacific are freshly silvered as, at Culpeper, Virginia, it heads south with Train 39, Washington to Atlanta, with coaches and Pullmans from Boston and Washington.

Lucius Beebe

GRIM-VISAGED GRANDEUR ON THE T. & P.

To complement the rolling oil smoke of the 900 Class Texas and Pacific 4-8-2
powering the North Texas Section of the Sunshine Special between Fort Worth
and Dallas the photographer has darkened the afternoon sky of Texas in a mood
of dark magnificence. Note the brass-capped stack, nickel-steel cylinder heads,
and burnished rod assembly of this famous class of T. & P. passenger engines.

Lucius Beebe

DAWN ON THE LACKAWANNA CUTOFF

The 1600 series of Delaware, Lackawanna and Western 4-8-4's are exceptionally well-proportioned Northern type freight engines. This one is wheeling a long string of redball freight westward at sunrise over the Lackawanna Cutoff at Andover, New Jersey, where the main line cuts east from the Delaware Water Gap. The Cutoff was built in 1911 when the road's finances were in bonanza and includes some of the heaviest viaducts and greatest fills known to railroading in America.

THIS WAS A STYLISH TRAIN

At Pine Bluff, Arkansas, this St. Louis–Southwestern Train No. 5, The Morning Star on the St. Louis-Texas run, possessed an added cachet of elegance in the form of two brass-platformed, spit-and-polish private cars, one the Fair Lane, occupied by Daniel Upthegrove, president and chairman of the board of the Cotton Belt, the other the Dixie, bearing the party of Judge Berryman Henwood, trustee of the railroad and its guiding legal genius. In addition to five head-end revenue cars, the sleek 4-8-2 No. 675 with its distinguishing Cotton Belt smokestack light, handrails, and smokebox-mounted bell, hauled a Pullman for Memphis, an attractive modern diner, and through streamlined coaches for Dallas. On a leisurely carding which allows approximately twenty-five hours for its run as against the speedier service of the Texas and Pacific, Missouri Pacific, and Frisco-Katy hook-ups between St. Louis and the Southwest, the Cotton Belt's route supplies an interesting and casual run through the little traveled rice fields of Arkansas and the oil and cotton regions of lower Arkansas and north Texas. Its finances restored and rendered prosperous by the wars, the St. Louis-Southwestern revitalized its services with such modern innovations as streamlined coaches, Diesel-electric motive power for freights, and the installation of Centralized Traffic Control over its busiest divisions.

Lucius Beebe

SLEEK MOTIVE POWER AND MANICURED ROADBED

From midcontinent fields, northeast to St. Louis and Kansas City, the largest revenue item on the Missouri-Kansas-Texas is oil with wheat, soft coal, and building merchandise contributing heavily to its income. Over the immaculately ballasted roadbed just north of Denison, Texas, a Mikado with trimly painted footboards is rolling this string of high cars and oil tanks north and will probably have them in the St. Louis yards the next morning. Spit and polish was a fetish with the Katy's progressive President Matthew Sloan and his engines, like the company's finances, are models of good maintenance.

C. M. Clegg

INTO THE SUNRISE AT DALLAS

With a long string of head-end revenue cars, coaches, and Pullmans picked up all the way from California, the Texas and Pacific's No. 6, the Texas Ranger, heads into the yards at Dallas, Texas. Its power is one of the T. & P.'s compact, chunky, and proverbially well-groomed Pacifics, No. 710, which will take the train through to Marshall, the terminal of the run, early in the afternoon.

Lucius Beebe

THE COTTON BELT'S LONE STAR

Train No. 1 of the St. Louis Southwestern, the Lone Star, on the overnight run between Memphis and Dallas with a Pullman, diner and coaches, makes up time on the southbound haul at Addison, a few miles north of Dallas. The motive power is one of the Cotton Belt's good-looking Mountain engines, No. 675, and the background is a field of the cotton from which the railroad takes its name.

Lucius Beebe

ONCE ALONG THE MONON

Now discontinued, but still a legend among the Illinois cornfields, the Chicago,
Indianapolis & Louisville's Tippecanoe once highballed every morning out of
the Dearborn Station on the Chicago-Indianapolis passenger run. A sleek little
varnish train, its consist usually comprised coaches, a diner, and a Pullman-
observation with the brass-railed rear platform of the old tradition. The Tippecanoe
is now with the snows of yesteryear, but here it is shown battling the snows of
not so many years ago during a January blizzard just south of Englewood depot,
Chicago.

Lucius Beebe

A STUDY OF LEHIGH VALLEY POWER

At Bound Brook, New Jersey, this westbound time freight with Mikado No. 470 on the smoky end neither paused nor posed for the cameraman, but nevertheless made a handsome study of Lehigh Valley tonnage rolling the high cars down the main line.

MIGHT ON THE MAIN LINE, TEXAS AND PACIFIC

C. M. Clegg

NO MISSING THE KATY SYMBOL

Across the green farmlands of Texas with the skyscrapers of Fort Worth in sight of the head-end crew, the Missouri-Kansas-Texas Train No. 27, the Blue-bonnet, St. Louis to Fort Worth and Dallas, is unmistakably a Katy undertaking. If the slotted sheet metal of its pilot and white trimmed footboards did not identify it, the Katy symbol on its tender, the M-K-T lettering on its characteristic yellow high car, an encore of the Katy shield on its other head-end revenue cars and legend on its coaches and diner would be sufficient. Like the solid black cabooses of the Rio Grande, the Tuscaned coaches of the Pennsy and the green and gold locomotives of the Southern, the Katy's bright yellow merchandise cars carried in most of its crack passenger consists are a hallmark of the railroad and a witness to the flair for promotion of the late Matthew Sloan, its resourceful president.

Lucius Beebe

A STUDY IN TEXAS AND PACIFIC POWER

C. M. Clegg

THE B. & O. CAPITOL LIMITED NEAR ABERDEEN, MARYLAND

DOUBLE-HEADER ON THE CENTRAL MAIN

Perhaps one of the New York Central's big Mohawks or one of the 6000 Series Niagaras could handle this train alone, but the urgency of the times has forced superintendents of motive power to use whatever comes to hand to keep the tonnage rolling, so two heavy-duty Mikados are blasting the skies with their exhausts ahead of this long drag of high cars eastbound a few miles west of Albany, New York.

4

THE PENNSY AND THE PACIFIC

AS WITH the Homeric legends and numerous other important matters in the realm of letters, history, and factual record, there is some divergence of opinion as to the origins of the Pacific or 4-6-2 type passenger locomotive and even more as to its name. It is known, for example, that in 1893 the Rhode Island Locomotive works designed and erected for the Chicago, Milwaukee and St. Paul Railroad three compound engines of this later almost universal wheel arrangement. Then in 1901 Baldwin built for the New Zealand Railways a series of locomotives of a similar type, according to Whyte's classification, and two years later American designed for the Missouri Pacific Railroad the first widely noticed 4-6-2 power to be used in this country. This is record, although, in an era when wide experimentation with types of wheel arrangements was in vogue, it is possible that some antecedent 4-6-2 engines predated even the first of these.

The origin of the name is much more open to speculation. It will be noted that in the case of the earliest of the locomotives listed above, those sold to the Milwaukee, the name Pacific was not then part of the incorporated title of the railroad although it became so a few years later. The second lot were designed and operated by an island subdivision of the then British Empire, now the British Commonwealth, and the association with the name Pacific is obvious. It is obvious, too, in the case of the passenger power built for the Missouri Pacific, much as with the Atlantic engine, first built by Baldwin in 1895 for the Atlantic Coast Line, and later types such as the Santa Fe, Union, Texas, and Hudson type engines.

It is possible, however, in view of the circumstances that in the mid-nineteenth century, when scarcely a railroad could be incorporated with any pretentions to respectability unless it included the word "Pacific," the engine type may have been named in honor of some ambitious railroad emerging from the swamps of Georgia or the coal hills of Pennsylvania with the hope of an ultimate Pacific coast terminus now forgotten and, sadly enough, unsung.

Whatever may be the facts of the matter, and they are, perhaps, no more than the proper concern of the sentimentalist and historian, the Pacific type engine for many years dominated the field of fast passenger motive power in North America and it is probable that its most celebrated redaction under the imprimatur of a single railroad has been the K-4s of the Pennsylvania. As this is being written the Pacific type engine is just a half-century old and the Pennsy's K-4s is rounding out a cycle of slightly more than thirty years' duration, and it seems a suitable subject, together with its antecedent and subsequently derived motive power along the main lines of that railroad, for some special consideration.

This engine was perfected and built in considerable numbers in 1914, was reproduced virtually without change in large orders in later years, and up until 1945 was the standard heavy-duty locomotive of the railroad for through passenger runs on fast schedules.

It has now been partially replaced by the larger and more powerful 4-4-4-4 type, Class T-1, which employs four cylinders and develops approximately 45 per cent more starting tractive effort (pull exerted on a standing train) than the K-4s; it is capable of more than twice the pulling power at speeds above 50 miles per hour. Fifty of the engines are being built, in addition to the two original T-1's which have been in service since 1942. In addition, the multi-cylinder locomotive fleet has been expanded by the acquisition of twenty-six 4-4-6-4 freight locomotives, Class Q-2, which are the most powerful engines in their working range ever built.

The K-4s engines faithfully carried the wartime load as the Pennsylvania moved what is by far the heaviest burden of military travel and essential civilian traffic it has ever known in the ninety-nine years of its history. During its long lifetime the K-4s has regularly powered the Broadway Limited, the Liberty Limited, the Spirit of St. Louis, the Trail Blazer, the Jeffersonian, the Cincinnati Limited, the Red Arrow, the General, the Admiral, the Gotham Limited, the Pennsylvania Limited, and a host of other Pennsylvania main-line trains, named and unnamed—pulling them all on fast schedules and, in later years, with trains vastly lengthened by the surge of wartime travel.

ARCHETYPE OF PENNSY POWER IN TANDEM

Two K-4s locomotives, specially assigned to the run of the Spirit of St. Louis as is indicated by the name plates under the road's identifying keystone, race eastward near Terre Haute, Indiana, with the road's crack varnish train on the St. Louis–New York run. It is possible that such crack runs may in future be powered by the Pennsylvania's newer Class T-1, four cylinder 4-4-4-4 engines, but the legend of the K-4s is assured of railroading immortality.

PENNSY POWER IN FORMAL DRESS

When the Pennsylvania dressed up a conventional K-4s Pacific in the stylish rig shown above to inaugurate the run a few years ago of the Jeffersonian, all-coach flyer on the New York–St. Louis run, it achieved one of the most successful of all essays in face-lifting for locomotives. The color scheme was black, silver and the Pennsy's own Tuscan red. Not so happy were the results with the two engines shown on the page opposite, both running on the head end of the Broadway Limited between New York and Chicago. They are similar except that the upper one has a less fully faired-in tender and lacks the flange on the airflow stack of the lower model. It also has the shield protecting its pilot coupling removed, achieving thereby a singularly untidy and unbuttoned appearance. With the exception of the handsome design above the Pennsy has been unfortunate in its gestures in the direction of modernizing the appearance of its K-4s engines.

C. M. Clegg

Courtesy of the Pennsylvania Railroad

Lucius Beebe

SYMMETRY AND SWIFTNESS: GG-1

The first electric locomotive on any American railroad to be streamlined and easily capable of hauling twenty steel passenger cars at 100 miles an hour, the Pennsylvania's Class GG-1 was originally designed for passenger traffic exclusively over the road's electrified divisions between New York, Philadelphia, Baltimore, Washington, and Harrisburg. Unforeseen urgencies of war years, however, so scrambled the uses of Pennsy motive power that steam and electric engines and motors, GG-1s, K-4s Pacifics, Mikados, Consolidations, P-5a electrics, M-1a Mountain jobs, and even the new Class S-1 with its novel 6-4-4-6 wheel arrangement were assigned at times in almost all conceivable combinations to all sorts of work. Here is a GG-1 on a local passenger haul near Lancaster, Pennsylvania.

Some of the east-west members of the Pennsylvania fleet have length-ened to the point where one K-4s cannot handle them on schedule, so that double-heading is frequently resorted to—underlining the need for the new T-1 locomotive, which provides sufficient power under one boiler to pull a full-length passenger train at speeds of up to 100 miles per hour, with energy still in reserve, and to handle freight trains at fast speeds as well. Its only assistant—except for the two T-1 engines, the "World's Fair" engine (the enormous 6-4-4-6 Pennsylvania type desig-nated Class S-1 that was on exhibition at the New York World's Fair in 1939 and 1940), and the brand new direct-geared steam turbine engine—has been a score or so of M-1 engines, the sturdy 4-8-2 freight and passenger unit developed by the P.R.R. in 1923, which are in regular passenger service.

The K-4s is handling trains at schedules never dreamed of when the engine was designed in 1914 and is operating over long distances. At Harrisburg, Pennsylvania, western terminus of the Pennsylvania's elec-trified territory, the steam locomotives take over from the huge GG-1 electric locomotives which bring the trains in from New York and Phila-delphia. Westbound trains leave Harrisburg behind engines which run through over the Middle and Pittsburgh divisions to Pittsburgh, a dis-tance of 245 miles. At Pittsburgh the four-track main line of the railroad divides—right in the station, incidentally—and one double-track portion heads for Chicago while the other two of the four tracks proceed to St. Louis.

All passenger engines are changed at Pittsburgh and, in the case of trains headed for Chicago, the fresh K-4s engine is used for the run to Crestline, Ohio, on the Eastern Division, a distance of 189 miles. Here a fresh engine takes over for the straightaway run over the fast Fort Wayne Division to Chicago, 280 miles away. A coal stop is made at Fort Wayne.

On the St. Louis line, the engine which hooks on at Pittsburgh runs through to Columbus, Ohio, on the Panhandle Division, a distance of 191 miles. At Columbus, the third engine takes over for the trip to St. Louis, stopping en route for coal at Eagle Creek and Effingham. This run is 420 miles. As an evidence of the utilization the railroad made of its K-4s engines during the war, it may be noted that many engines made a round trip over the Columbus and St. Louis Divisions between St. Louis and Columbus, approximately 840 miles, in a single day, and repeated the performance day after day.

The K-4s Class was developed to meet the need for a locomotive of materially greater power than the Atlantic (Class E-6s) or Pacific (Class K-2s) types in general passenger service on the Pennsylvania prior to 1914. The introduction of the steel passenger car had resulted in heavier trains, and the need for an engine which could maintain fast schedules without double-heading had become acute.

The genesis of the K-4s is to be found in three locomotives—the K-2, the K-3s and the E-6s. The "s" in Pennsylvania classification numbers indicates that the locomotive uses superheated steam. It has been allowed to fall into disuse in the railroad's own lexicon in recent years since super-heating has been a feature of all locomotives. Superheating effects an economy in steam consumption per horsepower-hour of approximately 30 per cent, and an increase of horsepower output, per locomotive unit, of 40 per cent.

The K-2 was designed by railroad engineers in Fort Wayne in 1910, and represented practically the maximum capacity then obtainable in a fast passenger locomotive using saturated steam, the superheater having not as yet been established in American locomotive design. A large number of these engines was built for service both east and west of Pitts-burgh. The wheel arrangement was 4-6-2, and the tractive force was 32,620 pounds. In appearance, the K-2 was somewhat similar to the present K-4s.

In 1913 the K-3s locomotive was evolved from the K-2. This new type was the K-2 partially redesigned to use superheated steam, with larger cylinders. Thirty K-3s engines were built in 1913 for service west of Pittsburgh. Tractive effort was 38,280 pounds.

While the K-2 was being developed, the Pennsylvania Motive Power Department was also busy producing an Atlantic type (4-4-2) passenger locomotive heavier than the E-2 and E-3 engines then in service. In 1910 this effort produced the first E-6 engine, an exceptionally powerful Atlantic type. This engine was thoroughly tested on the Pennsylvania

THE CLASSIC K-4s

Starting south out of Chicago at the head of the Liberty Limited, this Pennsy Pacific has an enlarged tender and a conventional pilot. Below is an identical locomotive snapped at the same spot on the mainline near Englewood but sporting a more modern, solid steel pilot with a drop coupling wheeling out the Broadway Limited, crack flyer on the Chicago–New York run.

locomotive test plant at Altoona, Pennsylvania, and on the road under actual operating conditions between Fort Wayne and Valparaiso, Indiana, a distance of 105 miles. It showed remarkable power and speed capacity, and proved to be equal to the larger K-2 at 40 miles an hour, and at higher speeds it developed more drawbar pull, so that it could pull any given train faster than the K-2. The same relation was found to exist between the E-6 and K-2 types when both were equipped with superheaters.

In 1912 the E-6 engine was partially rebuilt and equipped with a superheater, and two other experimental heavy Atlantic types were built. The next year the three engines were rebuilt into the final E-6s type, which has proved to be one of the most successful engines of American design. Eighty more E-6s engines were built in 1914, and the type is still employed on a number of divisions of the Pennsylvania in hauling shorter trains on fast schedules.

Those features of the Class E-6s engine which had been largely responsible for its success were incorporated in the K-4s when that design was worked out in 1914 to give the railroad a more powerful engine than either the K-2s or the E-6s. In fact, the K-4s is practically the highly efficient E-6s lengthened out sufficiently to accommodate a third pair of drivers, with the cylinders enlarged from 23½ x 26 inches to 27 x 28 inches, and with the boiler dimensions increased accordingly. These changes raised the tractive force to 44,460 pounds, an increase of 42 per cent as compared with the E-6, and of 36 per cent as compared with the K-2.

The K-4s boiler—the "heart" of any steam locomotive—is of the Belpaire type, with an inside diameter of 76⅝ inches. There are 236 ¼-inch tubes and forty 5½-inch superheater flues, all nineteen feet long. In each of the forty 5½-inch superheater flues are placed 1½-inch tubes, through which the steam flows to become superheated. The firebox measures 126 x 80 inches, the grate area is 70 square feet, the water heating surface 4,041 square feet, and the superheating surface 943 square feet.

A measure of the thoroughness of the design of the engine is to be

ON THE HORSESHOE CURVE

The signal bridge to the west of Kittanning Point station was the vantage point from which the photographer snapped this Pittsburgh local westbound on the Pennsy's four-lane highway around Horseshoe curve. Burgoon's Run is to the photographer's right and the body of water barely visible in the background is the City of Altoona's reservoir. Most heavy trains are double-headed through here but this light consist drifts along easily enough behind one of the road's great stable of M-1 locomotives, which sometimes pinch-hit for a brace of the lighter K-4s class.

found in the care taken to reduce weight wherever possible to increase efficiency. Thus, the axles, crank pins, wrist pins and piston rods are all hollow-bored. It is interesting to note that, in following its long-established policy of standardization of equipment, the Pennsylvania used many of the components of the K-4s in developing its Mikado freight engine, designated as type L-1s. The same boiler was used in both designs, as were certain other parts.

On the Altoona testing plant, where locomotives are run in a stationary position with the driving wheels turning on rolls which may be braked to reproduce the weight of a train, as though the engines were in actual service, the first K-4s locomotive developed a maximum of 3,184 indicated horsepower. Its starting tractive force is 44,460 pounds. After the original K-4s had been thoroughly tested, both on the test plant and on the road under actual operating conditions, it was duplicated in large numbers. Many more have been built in subsequent years, practically without change in design—proof of the correctness of the original engineering. At the present time, 424 of the engines are in service.

During the years immediately preceding World War II, experiments were made in streamlining the K-4s, and two designs were developed and applied to existing engines. The first of these was a complete "airflow" styling built along aerodynamic lines and giving the locomotive a sleek and bullet-like appearance. The other design was of a more practical nature and altered the appearance of the locomotive less conspicuously.

The electrification of the Pennsylvania Railroad between New York, Philadelphia, Baltimore, and Washington, and between Philadelphia, Lancaster, and Harrisburg, released many K-4s locomotives which had been hauling trains over the New York, Maryland, and Philadelphia divisions. Some of the released engines were placed in service west of Harrisburg, augmenting the locomotive fleet there, while the rest were placed in storage. It was these stored engines which provided the Pennsylvania with the margin of safety to be called upon when the enormous increase of military and essential civilian travel began to place troop trains on the railroad in ever growing numbers, and stretched out the regular trains until extra sections were called for.

Esthetically and to admirers of railroad locomotive power, the Class K-4s is perhaps the most satisfactory, to the visual senses, on the Pennsylvania's roster of either freight or passenger engines. Its simplicity of outward design, its alert poise and generally harmonious lines from smokebox to backhead give it a particularly handsome and—to indulge what may be a mere literary fancy—youthful appearance. About the only decorative note the railroad has ever approved, aside from the faired-in sheathing mentioned above and occasional experiments in smoke-deflecting devices of continental appearance, has been the traditional red lacquer keystone emblem bearing the gold-embossed serial number of the locomotive and mounted under the headlight on the smokebox. On some name-trains of the company's special pride, such as the New Yorker, Broadway Limited, and Spirit of St. Louis, the name of the train to which the individual engine was assigned has been added.

Whether or not the K-4s, to the eye of an *aficionado* concerned alone for harmony of proportions and symmetry of outline, would stand comparison with such famously beautiful locomotives as, say, the Daylight 4-8-4s of the Southern Pacific, the Texas and Pacific's 900 Series 4-8-2s, or the immaculately groomed passenger motive power of the Frisco in several classes, is problematical. Certainly, however, even a devotee of such striking thoroughbreds as the Reading's light Pacifics or the stream-lined Hudsons assigned to the Empire State Limited is moved by the sight of a tandem of the Pennsy's K-4s, fresh from the backshops, their paint jobs flashing under a noontide sun as they reel off the Indiana divisions at eighty miles an hour on the head end of the Jeffersonian, leaving a trail of flat black smoke over the farmlands to mark their going.

Lucius Beebe

C. M. Clegg

5
COLORADO CHRONICLE

FOR THE railroad *aficionado* the mountain magnificences and rolling uplands of Colorado offer a double miracle. For the student of legend, the archeologist whose concern is only for the record, it is peopled with the ghosts of the heroic past, a never-again land of wistful last chapters. For the student or pilgrim to whom the present is its own wonder and justification it is a place of bounce and vitality. The South Park's remembered whistles echoing through the night of Gunnison and Leadville are drowned in the reciprocating thunder of the Rio Grande wheeling its mighty tonnage over the Moffat or the Burlington, whose steel viastructure reaches from the Gulf of Mexico almost to the Dominion of Canada.

But to the person of sensibilities the past is too immediate to be ignored and the present is too inseparably a part of the past. The little engines standing forever between nowhere and nowhere, the tracks torn up behind them and before, at Idaho Falls and Central City, at Alamosa and Colorado Springs, are memorials to the great days, and great days dawned with only yesterday's sunrise. And in only yesterday's noontide there was fire under their crownsheets and a gloved hand on the throttle. Like the long-buried king and builder in the Kipling poem, they seem to say: "Tell him, I too, have known!"

What is true and characteristic of the spacious American West is true in double measure in Colorado. Suburban and gaudy doings transpired there within the memory of the still living generation, and to this day there are great bears along the Wolf Creek highway in winter, the drunken Indians sleep in the Saturday night gutters adjacent to the Strater Hotel in Durango, avalanches wash out the narrow-gage tracks into Silverton, and angry gentlemen in tailcoats still, as of only a few years since, at least, discharge pistol slugs into each other in the bar of the Brown Palace in Denver City. Gold is placered from the not too reluctant reaches of Clear Creek, claim jumping is still the moral equivalent of horse stealing in other parts of the West, and rich veins are uncovered right in the middle of the main street of Black Hawk. The spirit of Spencer Penrose, who took umbrage when the management of the Antlers in Colorado Springs asked him to leave for shooting glasses out of the hands of bar patrons and built the rival and stately Broadmoor—where, presumably, he could burn powder in whatever direction he pleased—is still abroad in the land.

Tarriers at the bar of the Windsor in Denver speak of Haw Tabor as though he had only a moment ago retired to his apartment on the second floor; every cab driver at the Union Depot is prepared on the raising of an eyebrow to convey customers to some lineal inheritor of the love store of Mattie Silk; the lustiest newspaper in the commonwealth achieved its prosperity on a basis of hilarious and unabashed blackmail; and in Central City there are still old-timers who recall how the Count Marat, the stylish barber, charged Horace Greeley five dollars for a shave and how Greeley, that very evening, quoted his immortal exhortation: "Go west, young man!" Uncle Horace was no fool and knew a land of opportunity when he saw one!

It is significant that Colorado's most distinguished man of letters of the current generation is the great Gene Fowler, a legendary character popularly reputed to have, in his mountain youth, preferred sticks of blasting gelatin when other tykes were licking candy canes and who, as a reporter on the Denver *Post*, engaged in salty backchat with Buffalo Bill Cody. Outraged by some reportorial impertinence, the mighty Pahaska thundered: "Young sir, my hairs are hoary!"

"Aye, sire," countered Fowler, "but not with eld!"

These are but ornaments to the pattern, embellishments of a vivid panorama, but the players in this allegory of bounce are the same who built the world's most spectacular railroads, who peopled their Palace cars with frock-coated sourdoughs capable of absorbing startling quantities of red-eye while their ladies sipped the best French champagne. There was a style and elegance to the territory and the later commonwealth. Colorado has never, to the reflective intelligence, been a vulgar place. In the legendary sixties when fresh fruits and vegetables were at a premium, an enterprising ruffian pushed a watermelon over the plains from Cheyenne to Denver in a wheelbarrow and, on the money realized from its auction, founded a considerable family and fortune. The Unsinkable Mrs. Brown, a parvenue who became one of the heroic figures of the *Titanic* disaster, is an integral part of the saga of the Queen City. Colorado has never been ashamed of realities.

The chronicle of Colorado railroading is more diffused and complex than most such records and is liberally illustrated with superlatives. Even in the minds of comparatively informed persons there is doubt as to what railroads were actually built and what ones existed only in name and on the parchments of their stock certificates. And so many of those that were, in fact, built and operated have been abandoned, that anyone but a railroad historian and specialist must pause before mentioning this or that narrow-gage line and recall its exact status of being, even as prudent citizens in the seventies of last century, before accepting a bank note, consulted a list of what banks were that week flourishing and what were defunct.

As recently as the early forties of the twentieth century the little cars of the Denver & Rio Grande Western's narrow-gage trains rolled north and south regularly between Santa Fe and Antonito, but today that division is only a fragrant memory. The famous Denver and South Park, long a household name throughout the railroading world, is with last year's snows. The lavishly planned and underwritten Denver and Laramie, whose tunnels were blasted and the right-of-way actually graded, never felt the impact of engine wheels or knew the passage of cars on its curves and tangents. In the Midland Terminal, running between Colorado Springs and Victor and Cripple Creek, can today be discerned the only remaining traces of the once mightily ambitious Colorado Midland which was to run through to the Pacific Coast. And even so knowing a Colorado historian as Gene Fowler himself recounts in *Timberline* how his one-time employers, Harry Tammen and Fred Bonfils, used to ride from Denver to Evergreen on the Pullmans of the Denver and Bear Creek. The record discloses there never was such a railroad!

The dominant characteristic of almost all Colorado railroading in the nineteenth century, like that of all the enterprises of the era, was one of speculation, bonanza and impermanence. In an age when silver was commonly used for pavements, barbershop floors, and the humblest household utensils and appointments, thousands upon thousands of miles of railroad, both narrow- and standard-gage, were projected, never in fact to operate. At one time there were so many railroads running into the boom town of Leadville that a traveler had a choice of four different approaches to the kingdom of Haw Tabor and his Matchless Mine, and the principal distinction between them was determined by the quality of the bourbon and the size of the portions of antelope steak served in their buffet cars. The South Park was reputed to maintain the most luxurious service out of Denver and the miners of the period favored it particularly because of the convenient racks for poker chips in the smokers and the presence of a massive safe for the accommodation of their surplus currency.

Narrow-gage travel in the Rockies was and is informal. Train crews were almost invariably armed and shot what game might be indicated by their pleasure or requirements along the right-of-way. As recently as the year 1945, the author has seen the rear brakeman of the Rio Grande Southern freight drag descend from the caboose at Placerville with a Winchester Express rifle in his hand and a small buck slung over his shoulder. Once, within a hundred feet of the engine cab in which he was riding on the standard-gage Laramie, North Park & Western, rolling through Windmill Hollow, he saw an enormous eagle swoop down and carry away a screaming snow rabbit to be consumed in full view on a nearby hilltop.

The advent of the railroads to Colorado in general and Denver in particular was conditioned by a number of circumstances political, financial and geographic, but fundamentally it was predicated on the existence of a single metal: gold. Their later histories were, to be sure, intricately involved in silver, coal, and more sophisticated mineral resources, but it was the dull red and infinitely persuasive grains in the gravel of the River Platte and Clear Creek and the bonanza legends of the Gregory Diggings at Central City and Black Hawk upon which rested the first basis for the loops and tangents, the grades, cuts, and fills of the high iron south of the Overland in Nebraska and Wyoming.

When Horace Greeley slammed down his roll-top desk in the old *Tribune* office at 154 Nassau Street, patted his disreputable white planter's hat into place, and set out to discover for himself what all the shouting was about in the ferocious reaches west of St. Louis, the first Overland Stage ferried him from Leavenworth to Denver in company of ten other passengers and eight guards armed to the whiskers with Sharp's rifles, Starr's Navy revolvers and Bowie knives. He had, of course, been preceded in 1858 by Uncle Dick Wooten who opened the town's first department store in an enchanting Niagara of Taos Lightning (a beverage so named because it was never necessary for it to strike in the same place twice); by William N. Byers, who had started the pungent and to this day animate *Rocky Mountain News*, and by the stylish Count Marat, who achieved as much fame wielding a razor as most of the great characters of history do waving swords, law books, or split infinitives. In addition to his better known advice on travel, Uncle Horace wrote of the other guests at his Denver hotel in 1859 that "they had a careless way when drunk of firing revolvers, sometimes at each other, at other times quite miscellaneously, which struck me as inconvenient for the quiet guest." Spencer Penrose, of a latter day Antlers and Broadmoor, had precedents for his target practice.

In these tumultuous times it was hoped by the citizens of Denver that the even then projected Pacific railroad, being surveyed by General Grenville M. Dodge, would pass through Denver and achieve its Salt Lake destination by any one of a number of considerable passes, the best known of which was the Berthoud. Half a decade of high hopes, executive bickering, and congressional backing and filling ended with the main line of the Union Pacific passing through neither Denver nor Salt Lake. John Evans, Colorado's territorial delegate to Washington, was as stunned and dismayed as was Brigham Young of the Latter Day Saints, and Denver business men and bankers were stowing their Gladstones and carpet bags aboard Ben Holladay's Overland coaches and lighting out for Julesburg, Cheyenne, and Laramie by the score. Back in New York, Thomas Durant, a vice-president of the swaggering Union Pacific, added insult to injury by remarking that "Denver is too dead to bury."

The record of the involved public events surrounding the genesis, construction, and final completion of the Denver Pacific Railway is more in the realm of financial reporting that that of the railroad historian.

THE GEORGETOWN LOOP

No student of railroading needs any identification of this spectacular and celebrated example of Colorado mountain railroad engineering. The High Bridge,
where engineers and sightseers alike delighted to pause to be photographed, is
at the lower right. The center track of the Colorado and Southern passes beneath its middle span and Georgetown itself is down the canyon over the right
shoulder of the reader. It was from this valley that both the C. & S. and the
Argentine Central once hoped to build through to Leadville, but today even
the rails and girders of the bridge are vanished and the C. & S. locomotives which
once traversed them are gone, some to Alaska and one each as memorials to the
communities of Central City and Black Hawk, motionless souvenirs of the great
days when their smoke ascended to timberline and the echo of their whistles was
abroad in the land.

"IN TELLURIDE, IN TELLURIDE,
I STRUCK IT RICH AND I FOUND MY BRIDE!"

Mining Town Ballad

This rare photograph by W. H. Jackson, taken near Lizard Head, shows locomotive No. 1 with a special train of two passenger cars bound, according to a contemporary caption, from Dolores to Telluride over the Rio Grande Southern, the loneliest and most desolate narrow-gage railroad in the United States. Its route was laid out by Otto Mears in the eighties when it was found impossible for the Denver & Rio Grande Western to continue its proposed route from Silverton to Ouray where the so-called Million Dollar Highway now serves as a motor road through the Uncompaghre Mountains.

DISASTER NEAR THE DIVIDE

At some remote date, to which the costumes of the spectators furnish the only clue, this Colorado Central (later C. & S.) narrow-gage locomotive seems to have left the straight and narrow without, however, apparently doing much damage to the track or roadbed. The scene is the outskirts of Central City in an age when Central was pleased to consider itself the metropolis of the "richest square mile in the world." It is safe to assume that traffic was resumed within a few hours.

SIGHTLY, STATELY, AND STANDARD GAGE

When the most famous of all Colorado photographers, W. H. Jackson, posed this Colorado Midland train for his wet plate camera on the high bridge near Buena Vista, the railroad was owned by the Santa Fe and was a serious rival to the expansive plans of the Denver & Rio Grande. Later the Colorado Midland was known as the largest railroad abandonment in the world and today its great tradition is carried on only by the Midland Terminal, a still vital and functioning ore and cattle haul road between Colorado Springs and Victor and Cripple Creek.

TERMINAL OF THE MIDLAND AT CRIPPLE CREEK

The depot, switches, and storage tracks of the Midland Terminal at Cripple Creek, showing the yards with a water tower and engine house in the background. A train a day now arrives and departs from this town where, in the nineties, the Gold Securities Exchange was the busiest block but where now the dust gathers on disused mining tools, and the once vibrant rails are grown with weeds.

The road—the moving geniuses of the building of which were George Francis Train, the eccentric railroad promoter, General William J. Palmer, who was borrowed from the Kansas Pacific to hasten the actual laying of the rails, and David H. Moffat, immeasurably the most distinguished railroad figure in the annals of the Centennial State—did not become an actuality until 1870. Train, a spellbinder of parts imported by the Denver Board of Trade during the height of its transportation crisis, got off to a wrong start when he told a meeting of first citizens that a railroad connecting the Queen City with Cheyenne would cost no more than the community spent for whisky and tobacco during a period of three years. The argument, which Train later admitted was not conceived in one of his most inspired moments, fell upon deaf and even hostile ears. Two million dollars' worth of whisky, it was generally conceeded, was substantial, even at the prevailing and exorbitant price of two bits a slug. When Train, however, perceiving the error of his statistics or at least their implication, remarked that adequate railroad facilities could hardly help resulting in a lowering of freight charges and that the price of best forty-rod Kentucky might reasonably be expected to reach the gratifying level of a dime, Denver was transported with enthusiasm and public spirited miners and other philanthropists subscribed the sum in what was widely described as a trice.

The *Daily Colorado Tribune* in an extra for June 28, 1870, somewhat dryly reported the great event in the following terms:

The first train over the Denver Pacific Railway arrived in Denver last evening, June 22, about seven o'clock, bringing Chicago papers of the 20th, and Omaha papers of the 21st. A large number of people were at the depot to witness the incoming of the train. Trains will leave regularly hereafter, each morning at 6:10, Denver time, and arrive at 7 P.M. Time on the road, about five hours; fare, ten dollars.

The track has been entirely completed with the exception of the laying of two or three rails, and the driving of the silver spike, which will take place on Friday morning. After the completion of the laying of the track, Mr. L. H. Eicholtz, the efficient Chief Engineer of the company, and Superintendent of construction, was invited to the general office of the company and presented with an elegant Elgin gold watch and chain by the officers of the road. Gov. Evans made a short speech complimenting Mr. Eicholtz on his energy, ability and gentlemanly bearing, and assuring him of the high appreciation the officers of the road had of his services. Mr. Eicholtz replied in a few words, expressing his opinion that his services had been overrated and his gratitude for the compliment paid him.

Twenty-nine years later, the pioneer W. N. Byers sat in Elitch's Gardens at a little green painted table and recalled, for a reporter from the Denver *Republican*, some rather more colorful details of the occasion.

Everyone in town was present [he said], whether or not the nature of their business made it suitable, and the ceremonies were held at the old station which had been itself finished about six months before the railroad was completed. Elaborate preparations had been made and a gold spike was to have been driven, but it was stolen before the time of the ceremonies came around, and a good, honest iron spike covered with yellow paper was driven in its stead. A passenger train came in the same day and after that service was continuous. The coming of the railroad, I may add, was not universally regarded as a good thing, and some people thought it would ruin the town and were strongly opposed to it.

Among those who did not think the railroad was a good thing were unquestionably the hard-boiled overland teamsters who had for years been freighting in Denver's consumer goods from Cheyenne and Evans and who were now doomed to professional oblivion, even as the coming of the railroads in upstate New York was the death warrant of the picturesque boatsmen along the canals.

Later in the same year the completion between Denver and Golden, a community which at the time was being variously promoted as the potential state capital and leading metropolis of the countryside, of twelve miles of the Colorado Central Railway, was an occasion which called for the accustomed speechmaking, rolling out of barrels, and contests between local fire companies—a form of communal endeavor which, in the seventies and eighties, far surpassed in excitements such later contests as baseball or basketball.

The most casual examination of the records of the period shows that conflagrations of dramatic if not actually catastrophic proportions were frequent occurrences and figured largely in the public prints. The entire community of Central City, for example, was in May of 1874 destroyed by a holocaust which prompted clergymen and editorial writers to compare it favorably to Nero's most celebrated essay in the field of pyromania. The devastation began in the humble premises of a China boy's laundry in Spring Street during the progress of what were darkly described by the press as "secret religious rites of oriental and un-Christian origin." As there was no fire company in Central and no pump works either, the fire was an almost total success and it was not for nearly a year that the town regained its former urban and architectural magnificence.

As a result, fire companies flourished on every hand. Probably Georgetown had more than most and even today at least half a dozen wagon houses and hose towers still stand in that community, wistful reminders of the brave days of silver trumpets, red flannel shirts, and the glories of Hope Hose No. 1. At a red letter day in local railroading, celebrating the acquisition, a few years later, of a new ten-ton locomotive for the Colorado Central's Clear Creek Lines, it was reported in the Georgetown *Miner* that the following fire companies participated in the civic sarabands:

> The Joe Bates Hose, Denver
> The Hope Hose No. 1, Georgetown
> The Rough and Ready Hook and Ladder, Central
> The Excelsior Hose, Golden
> The Alpine Hose, Golden
> The Georgetown Fire Company No. 1
> The Rescue Hose, Central
> The Pueblo Civic Hose

It was while a spirited sprinting-against-time contest was in enthusiastic progress at this festival and while Viol's Cornet Band and the Fife and Drum Corps of the Emerald Rifles were dislodging boulders from crags in the adjacent canyons with their deathless harmonies, that "a vile cur ran between the legs of Mr. Jones of the Pueblo Hose and tripped him, but he threw himself beyond the wheels and fortunately escaped injury." Concussions sustained beneath the wheels of speeding fire apparatus were as commonly incidental to Fourth of July, barn raisings, and railroad dedications as powder burns and alcoholism.

There was a strong bond between the fire fighters and the railroaders who, as often as not, were responsible for their most gaudy and successful conflagrations, and "the firing of cannon, sweet strains of music and clangor of alarm bells" were accepted accompaniments of all golden spike drivings.

Moffat's success with the Denver Pacific served to encourage the pioneer to further endeavor in the form of the construction of the Florence and Cripple Creek and South Park lines. In 1872 the Santa Fe had laid its rails as far as the Colorado boundary, the Rio Grande became its principal competitor and the railroad building era of Colorado began its fullest flowering. As a matter of record, too, the era of railroad abandonments set in while promoters were still envisaging countless thousands of as yet unsurveyed rights-of-way. Only seven years elapsed between the entry of the first railroad into Denver and the abandonment of the Arkansas Valley, an affiliate of the Kansas Pacific running in actual operation between Kit Carson and La Junta and graded somewhat farther west with the intention of crossing the Rockies.

No commonwealth ever boasted such a multiplicity and wide variety of ground breakings, golden spike layings, and first trains as Colorado. For three decades the territory and later state were a lush field for the enterprise of bunting salesmen, public orators, and proprietors of the noisier order of brass bands. Excursions and jollifications were the order of the day among the citizens of an extremely hard-working and proportionally hard-drinking frontier.

When the Colorado Central was completed as far as Golden "the event gave pleasure and satisfaction to all portions of Colorado," according to the *Rocky Mountain News* for September 27, 1870.

There were three excursion trains from Denver during the day, the ride being free to all. The crowd went on the 12 o'clock train, which was accompanied by the G.A.R. Band, the Cornet Band having gone up in the mountains. It was composed of six cars drawn by the engine "Golden" which was most handsomely decorated with flags and wreathes of evergreen. After a rapid and pleasant ride, the train arrived at Golden, and rolled up to the depot amid loud cheers, the firing of cannon and small arms and the sweet strains of music.

As was customary, since the historic precedent the year previous at Promontory, two spikes, one of gold and one silver, were driven, a teamster was painfully but not fatally injured by gunfire during the dedicatory speech of the Honorable W. A. H. Loveland, the president of the road, and an unidentified character with lamentable lack of manners contrived to get one leg into the barrel of Daniel Webster punch which the directors provided for the occasion.

These stately and even pontifical occasions almost invariably suffered

Lucius Beebe

COLORADO AND SOUTH-EASTERN

The Colorado and South-Eastern is a little known coal haul road with four miles of ancient rails between Ludlow and Delagua but with trackage rights over the Colorado and Southern to Trinidad. This is its one engine in operating condition with its daily drag of empties, but in the ruined and windowless stalls of a decaying roundhouse at Delagua are the hulks of several other old-timers stripped of their rods and useful running parts to sustain the road's one practicable engine in its senescent age. The mines served by the C. & S.-E. produce thirty or forty cars of coal a day which drift down the grade to Trinidad and are hauled back empty with great labor on the part of No. 2.

Lucius Beebe

LAST TRACE OF A ONCE MIGHTY EMPIRE

With the thermometer registering below zero early of a February morning, a Midland Terminal drag with a Consolidation at either end thunders into the Colorado mountain passes near Divide. The Midland Terminal, actually no terminal railroad at all, is the standard-gage survivor of the three railroads which once entered Cripple Creek and one of the most spectacular standard-gage examples of railroad construction in the world. Before passenger service was discontinued some years ago it was famous for its sightseeing cars, some of which, in humbler circumstances, can still be seen along its right-of-way.

Lucius Beebe

FIT FOR THE EASTER PARADE

Between Trinidad and Tercio (logically enough by way of Primero and Segundo) in Colorado just north of the New Mexican boundary runs a division of the Colorado & Wyoming, a railroad with the best maintained motive power in the Southwest. Its shops at Segundo, complete to the last hydraulic jack, lathe, and hoist, glitter with precision tools like a watchsmith's. Its two beautiful little engines, engaged in hauling a daily coal drag down to Trinidad for the mighty Colorado Fuel and Iron Company, are resplendent in silver paint with green trim and might have just been wheeled out of Tiffany's show rooms. One of the two Consolidations which are the pride of their crews is usually being shopped while the other is working steam. When General Palmer was laying out the "camino de fiero caril" which he planned for this old Spanish region, the demand of local property owners that the railroad be constructed near their mines and ranches required the promising of numerous branch lines, and the Southern Division of the Colorado & Wyoming is one of these.

"THE STORY OF AMERICA IS WRITTEN IN ITS HOTELS"

Gene Fowler

In an age when Colorado railroads handed around free passes of solid silver which cost ten dollars apiece to fabricate at Tiffany's in New York and when bar-room floors were frequently paved with silver dollars laid edge to edge, Georgetown was celebrated for three things: the Georgtown Loop of the Colorado and Southern Railroad, the multiplicity of its fire companies, and Louis du Puy's Hotel de Paris and French Restaurant. Erected in 1875 in Alpine Street next door to McLellan's Opera, French Louis' was the most famous and by long odds the most luxurious dining room in Colorado, transcending in bright renown even Haw Tabor's favorite Saddle Rock at Leadville, a premises which boasted a chef from Delmonico's! Louis' special guests such as Madam Janauschek, were served their quail and reindeer and eastern terrapin off Haviland china in the library whose walls were crowded with French classics in Riviere bindings. His champagne was served in crystal chalices which held an even litre apiece and his cognac bore the fabled imprimatur of the Comet Year, 1811. Broadcloth coated notables from Denver, Tom Walsh, old Charlie Boettcher, Jack Morrisey, slept comfortably on the Colorado and Southern's red plush seats on the return trip, in happy trances induced by Louis' sheep's feet, *sauce soubise, omelette aux champignons*, and vintage Burgundies. French Louis hated his guests, according to the legend, but his ghost still haunts Georgetown and perhaps his patrons do too: the Grand Duke Alexis, George Pullman, the Carrolls of Carrollton, Bayard Taylor, Henry M. Stanley, who in another world may exclaim: "Louis du Puy, I presume?"

"IN A LAND OF SAND AND RUIN AND GOLD"

Swinburne's *"The Triumph of Time"*

From Denver south through Colorado Springs, Pueblo, and Walsenburg to Trinidad, the Burlington, through the agency of the Colorado and Southern and Fort Worth and Denver City, has trackage rights over the same iron with the D. & R. G. W. and, as far as Pueblo, the Santa Fe. Over this main artery to the deep southwest the Burlington rolls two passenger trains daily in each direction and a considerable tonnage of freight, Texas-bound, as is shown behind this 2-10-2 flying white flags and racing southward near Wigwam, Colorado.

"SHE WHISTLED ONCE AT THE WHISTLING POST AND THEN FLASHED BY LIKE A FRIGHTENED GHOST!"

George Milburn

Upper left: Lucius Beebe

One of Colorado's little exploited steam railroads whose network of trackage connects the parent company's several sugar mills with the Union Pacific and Colorado and Southern is the Great Western. Its home offices, shops, roundhouse, and yards are at Loveland, and revenue passengers, something of an oddity nowadays, may ride its well-kept cabooses. Most of its motive power is of the Consolidation class and here is shown No. 51, flying white as it rolls southward near Longmont.

HEADED FOR THE ROUNDHOUSE STALL

Lower left: C. M. Clegg

Consolidation No. 60 of the Great Western, with a cut of high cars and a plume from its smokestack, heads out of Officer for the home terminal of Loveland. The bulk of the railroad's traffic is in the raw material and products of its parent organization, the Great Western Sugar Company, but it is a common carrier and all sorts of freight can be found in its several daily scheduled hotshots among the plain cities of northern Colorado.

Lucius Beebe

A PASTORAL IN WINTRY COLORADO

This low-wheeled Mikado with a snow shield bolted to its pilot beam and high coal boards topping its tender is the pride of the Laramie, North Park & Western Railroad, a Union Pacific feeder serving the North Park district of Colorado and connecting with the U. P. main line at Laramie, Wyoming. No. 3 is shown with a mixed consist—revenue passengers may ride in the caboose—against a background of the Snowy Range. The spark arrester, which contains three separate wire cinder filters, is for the protection in summertime of the heavily forested uplands the road traverses on its way to Walden and Coalmont.

C. M. Clegg

UNION PACIFIC SUPERPOWER ROLLS TOWARD DENVER

C. M. Clegg

SHADOWS AMONG THE SAGEBRUSH

Rarest of all collector's items in the domain of Colorado railroading is the San Luis Valley Southern, a thirty-five mile agricultural line running south from Blanca, where it meets the Denver and Rio Grande Western's right-of-way between Alamosa and Walsenburg, to Jaroso on the New Mexico border. This altogether enchanting picture of the archetype of short-line railroading shows the S. L. V. S.'s Consolidation No. 104 (the company has two other steam locomotives) approaching its terminal at sundown ahead of the coach which serves as passenger, baggage, mail and business car on this lonely run in the shadow of the Culebra Mountains.

C. M. Clegg

PRIDE AND POLISH ON THE DENVER & SALT LAKE

C. M. Clegg

IN THE SHADOW OF PIKE'S PEAK

At Midland, Colorado, three-quarters of a mile above its terminal roundhouse at Colorado Springs and with Pike's Peak towering against a cobalt winter sky a few miles to the east, the Midland Terminal's No. 60, a low-wheeled Consolidation, halts at the head end of a freight consist to take on water for the final haul over the breathless grades to Victor and Cripple Creek. Around the curve, as the fireman peers out, oil can in hand, is a pusher of the same type. Note the coal board on the tender and the tractive power implicit in the heavily counterbalanced low-drivers.

"THE PLOUGHMAN HOMEWARD PLODS HIS WEARY WAY AND LEAVES THE WORLD TO DARKNESS..."

Gray's "Elegy"

The rotary plow of the Laramie, North Park & Western Railroad at the end of a long day in the mountain passes of the Snowy Range of Wyoming and Colorado, heads for the Laramie roundhouse. The picture was taken at Windmill Hollow, Wyoming, as the North Park's stout little Mikado trails two crummies, one bearing the road's own insignia, the other a Union Pacific cookshack and bunkhouse, as it noses the big rotary along with a full crew of eight men to watch for rocks and operate the two engines. Drifts thirty feet deep through which they must tunnel are not uncommon in the winter lives of these railroaders.

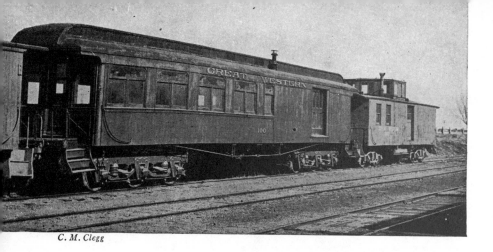

C. M. Clegg

DREAMING OF THE STORIED PAST

At Loveland yards, the Great Western's sole remaining combination baggage, coach, and observation car rests out the years while the few remaining passengers the line carries ride in the cabooses of freight trains. No. 100 is not, however, totally neglected in its old age and is in a fair state of preservation. Note the six-wheel trucks sufficient for a car twice its weight.

Scribner's Magazine 1888

WINTER IN THE MARSHALL

At Gunnison, Colorado, is the largest roundhouse filled with narrow-gage engines anywhere in America. There the Rio Grande stables its iron ponies for the run over the Marshall Pass into Salidia. In winter the snow drifts into the Marshall thirty and forty feet deep and the motor highway over the adjacent Monrach Pass is often closed for days at a time despite the efforts and modern machinery of the Highway Patrol. Over this wild and desolate stretch of track the Rio Grande's freights, single-engined out of Gunnison, are double-headed and sometimes triple-shotted for the 10,800 foot pass. The helper engines are stationed at Sargents where the highway and the railroad separate to go over the mountains. In the eighties and nineties it sometimes required eight or even ten narrow-gage engines to push the heavy rotaries and wedge plows over the hill, and tying down the hand brakes on high cars during the Colorado blizzards was no small task. Here a head shack of the era "decorates" the tops in a contemporary drawing.

from minor contretemps which passed more or less unnoticed in the spacious customs of the times, but which the reporters of trivialia have recorded for the harmless pleasure of posterity. At Promontory, in 1869, it did not pass without notice that due perhaps to the heady excitements of the moment, perhaps to the resources of Central Pacific President Stanford's private car, none of the eastern notables on hand were able to hit the golden spike with any satisfactory degree of precision and that it was finally driven home by a professional railroad man. At the opening of the Denver Pacific, as recorded previously, some knave or lout had made away altogether with the golden spike. At almost all of these civic occasions the cynical enquirer into the record of the day can discover the activity of some misguided enthusiast who fell under the wheels, took pot shots at the polished silk dicers of the guests of honor, or contrived to set fire to an adjacent and happily inflammable edifice.

When, in 1881, the narrow-gage tracks of the Rio Grande were completed as far as Durango, a community more celebrated for its gusty way of life than its meticulous devotion to protocol, the program committee overlooked a few details of hospitality, a circumstance which seemed to depress nobody in the least degree.

At 5:45 last evening [recalled the Denver *Daily Republican* in a dispatch datelined Durango, August 7], the special train containing the Colorado excursionists, which had been delayed by the washouts near Navajo, arrived in this city. The dangerous places on the road had been cribbed up and made as safe as possible, but even then the rails curved and sank several inches beneath the weight of the train, at one time threatening to throw the engine into a creek below. Fortunately, owing to the presence of mind of Engineer Hoag, the locomotive and train passed over safely and any possible accident was averted. It is needless to say that the excursionists disembarked and walked over the majority of those dangerous places, only resuming their places in the cars when all danger had been passed. No delay occurred between Navajo and Durango and the entire party arrived at the latter place tired out, but greatly pleased at reaching their destination. There was no formal reception at the depot, but one was tendered the delegation at six o'clock at one of the hotels....

"The cities of Colorado, the oldest and the newest," was answered by Mayor Sopris, of this city, who spoke of Denver and Durango, and showed how the interests of both were mutual.

"Leadville, the fastest city in the Union," was ably taken care of by Mayor Dougan, who extended the right hand of friendship to the citizens of Durango, and made some other appropriate and well-worded remarks. He denied the soft impeachment that Leadville was "fast."

"The San Juan country," was answered by Mr. M. J. McKenna, of Moline, Illinois, an extensive mine owner; while "The mining and smelting interests of the San Juan," brought Mr. J. A. Porter, of the San Juan smelting works to his feet. Ex-Governor Gilpin replied to the toast, "The pioneers of Colorado," and Messrs. J. E. Waters and Mr. Spence of Rico, acknowledged the obligation to "The mining engineers," and "The narrow gauge engineers," respectively.

The programme arranged for the banquet was considerably curtailed owing to the lateness of the hour. After the banquet, the excursionists retired to secure their first sleep for three nights; but, owing to the crowded condition of the hotels, accommodations were rather limited, and the members of the delegation who were last to arrive in the city suffered in consequence, many of them sleeping in chairs. The proprietors, however, did everything in their power to accommodate their guests, and they are highly spoken of by all who came in contact with them.

Among these splendors of musketry, oratory, and the execution of spirited municipal rigadoons, there were, of course, comparatively sober and discerning spectators of the progress of the rails who, once the smashed hats had been swept from the scene and the fire companies had hammered out the dents in their silver trumpets, essayed to survey the railroad prospect with a gaze focused to more enduring contentments and satisfactions. The enchantments of carnival commanded public attention and, certainly, participation, but Colorado didn't for a moment lack the shrewd sense which told it that the spiked iron was much more than an occasion for the superlatives of spellbinders.

Let us, in a gentler vein, follow the reporter of the *Rocky Mountain News* in an anabasis to Central City over the newly completed narrow gage and set in Pioneer Byers' best type for the issue of November 26, 1872, remembering always that newswriting then was a synthesis of factual reporting and editorial expression no longer encountered in sophisticated dailies.

We rode today [the reporter wired under a Central City dateline] for the first time over the narrow gauge division of the Colorado Central railroad. The run from Golden to "end of track" was made in about two hours and a half; being at the rate of eight miles per hour. The train consisted of locomotive and tender, baggage car and passenger coach. The latter is a very handsome and elegant car, from the Omaha car shops of the Union Pacific company. It is the same size and very much like the coaches of the Rio Grande. Today it was crowded full of passengers. The baggage car is also new but considerably smaller and not so well finished as those on the Rio Grande road. The engine is not near adequate to its work; being one of the machines built for and used in grading the approaches to the Omaha bridge over the Missouri. It is a rude, roughly made engine and its power was taxed to the utmost on the steeper grades. Three of these engines are in use, but much of their time is necessarily employed in bringing forward construction material. Better engines are expected before long. Probably they have not been procured sooner because the company wanted first to experiment and determine what power it would be necessary to get. Certainly they must be satisfied by this time that motive power greatly in excess of the common proportion will be necessary to operate the road successfully. Either trains will have to be short and light, the locomotive very strong and heavy, or else used in twos and threes. The grade is very steep—in some places exceeding two hundred feet to the mile for short distances. The difficulty of surmounting it is greatly augmented by the almost constant curvature of the track. Very little is straight. Reverse curves succeed one another as continuous as the track of a snake.

Generally speaking the road-bed is first class. In a few places very high water may encroach upon it, but there cannot be much damage from that source. Almost continuously it is supported on the side toward the stream by a retaining wall of stone laid up without mortar, and varying from five to thirty feet in height. In the beginning, some of these were built too near perpendicular. Most such have been rebuilt, and all are now very substantial. It is the best tied road we ever saw. The surface is fully half covered with them, and the rails are very securely fastened. The tracks is yet rough, every energy having been bent to its extension. Very little has been done at aligning or leveling it up since the track-layers left it.

Passengers were carried today to a point within two miles of the city limit of Black Hawk. Tomorrow the transfer will be made at the mouth of Smith Hill gulch. Graders are scattered all along from that point to Black Hawk. Probably they number two hundred—blasting rocks, digging and wheeling dirt. The railway destroys the wagon road, following directly in it most of the way. A bridge to be built just below Black Hawk will probably delay the track somewhat, but it will be in the town before the date stipulated in the contract for county bonds January 1, 1873.

Altogether this section of road is a great accomplisment; great in the fact itself, but greater as the first successful experiment in building over ground that until this trial would have been considered totally impracticable as a railway route, for the double reason of its steepness and tortuous pathway. Properly finished and with rolling stock adapted to its requirements there is no reason why it may not be operated with entire success, though a competing line over more favorable ground would of course have an advantage over it. Of course with age it will have many improvements. The heavy grades will be cut down and the curves lengthened.

The scenery from Golden to Central is without comparison in railway travel. For stupendous heights and wild grandeur, the railroad world cannot produce its like. In the spring and summer seasons, when Vasquez river will be at the flood and its tributaries are pouring in cascades down the mountain sides, it will alone be worth a journey across the continent to see.

Accidents of all degrees of seriousness were frequent in the early annals of Colorado railroading, a circumstance which might abundantly be expected from the nature of the terrain traversed, the imperfections of technique, and the haste and excitements of the times. Construction was often accomplished in a rough and ready manner which would give twentieth century engineers the vapors; official locomotive and boiler inspection was practically non-existent, and highly individualized operations had yet to give way to the uniformity and discretion of train orders, signals, and dispatching.

As early as 1872 the Denver *News* chronicled on May 28th and in an entirely matter-of-fact way, that a Colorado Central engineer, on looking back over his train near Boulder, had noted the absence of eight of his ten cars of mixed freight and passengers and had at length discovered them intact at the bottom of a four-mile grade where they had rolled when he had inadvertently pulled a drawbar.

Far less reassuring were the details of a savage wreck on the Colorado Midland in 1891 at Aspen when two passengers of a "laundry" or excursion train were killed outright and eight others cooked to subsequent death by escaping steam. The Midland's engine, No. 22, involved in this wreck, was generally considered the line's bad luck locomotive and was responsible, aside from the fatalities of the Aspen wreck, for the loss of twenty-one lives before it was at last junked.

Derailments, runaways, boiler explosions, and the occasional loss of locomotives and even whole trains over mountainsides were by no means uncommon. The only engine then in operating condition on the Gilpin County Tramway rolled off the rails at Black Hawk in 1892 and all service was suspended on the line while it spent a fortnight in the shops. When, in 1945, a "Galloping Goose" on the Rio Grande Southern ran away for a distance of twelve miles down the slopes of Dallas Divide and finally stopped in a meadow with no harm done, the only surprise voiced in the local press was at the good condition of the rails and roadbed which had permitted so wild a run without wrecking the vehicle involved.

Less under the head of accidents, although possibly, as far as Phineas Barnum was concerned, an act of God, was the occasion in the seventies when the circus train became stalled on the tracks of the South Park while climbing over Boreas pass, 11,500 feet above sea level, between Como and Breckenridge.

Dexter Fellows, greatest of all circus press agents, had not yet emerged to fame and it may be taken at the word of W. D. Penny, then an engineer on the South Park, that a fouled injector caused his little Consolidation to die on him a few thousand yards east of the Continental Divide which marked the top of the three and a half per cent grade. There were three cars of animals between his drawbar and the caboose, all of them hungry, the lions especially so, and night was coming on. The tigers were outraged and there was muttering among the panthers but, Mr. Penny later recalled, it was the roaring of the lions that caused him most uneasiness. What if they should contrive to escape and start up the narrow ledge which supported the track? An engineer would be the merest hors d'oeuvre to them! Besides, the track was one way and the down trains loaded with ore were waiting!

It was at this point that the chief mahout of elephants, his wits doubtless quickened by the terrors of this fearful farland and anxious for the amenities of what passed for civilization, was seized of an inspiration. His docile and well-mannered charges were led from their car and two of the most ponderous stationed with what-next expressions on their foreheads against the rear of the caboose. Penny whistled off his brakes, the head shack gave him a highball, the fireman uttered a silent prayer and recalled a few carnal offenses against heaven, the mahouts swore in Arabic, the lions roared like senators at an appropriations hearing, and the elephants heaved mightily!

The arrival of the train with its uncommon rear-end motive power at Breckenridge was sensational. A number of tarriers in the El Dorado, Last Chance, and Hurry Back saloons, summoned by the excited shouts of the observers, took one look at the cavalcade and hastily sought safety among the bronze cuspidors with terrified assertions that they had seen elephants. The motive power superintendent of the South Park was troubled with dreams that night that his roundhouses had all been remodeled for the accommodation of pachyderm motive power.

The circus train from Como became a legend.

The record shows that, so delighted were the miners of the day by the elephants' exploits that later, at Leadville, a fellow of good intentions but essentially unsound mind, introduced a quantity of Leadville Mule, a highly esteemed local beverage, into their supper mash and that, for a time, in hell there was nothing like it. As late as the era of national prohibition Leadville Mule was celebrated in Colorado and passed as a form of almost universally accepted currency. Thomas Ferril, a contemporary historian, recalls that it traveled the narrow gage, then Colorado and Southern, in the baggage cars in ten-gallon milk containers and was accepted and delivered as the most accustomed legal merchandise.

Narrow-gage travel in the late seventies was by no means confined to coaches, and the Palace cars with "velvet seats and silver trim in liberal quantities" which had so aroused the editorial admiration of the *Daily Colorado Tribune* when the standard-gage Denver Pacific first came to town, were very soon reproduced in luxurious miniature on the strait gage. When the South Park was pushing its way through Platte Canyon and over Kenosha Hill at 10,000 feet, paying its way during the years of its construction and paying dividends at the same time, nothing was too good for voyagers to the new El Dorado. The miners, it is recorded, particularly enjoyed the buffet dining cars with their alcoves, intimately shielded from the public gaze by looped and fringed drapes and corded upholstery where jackets and tailcoats could be discarded without offense to ladies during an all-night poker session crossing the Divide.

Jay Gould was inspecting the road in the late seventies with an eye to its possible purchase and Edith B. Townsend later recalled that, as a little girl, she traveled with him on the first narrow-gage Pullman out of Denver. He was delighted with the admiration excited by the nickel, mirrors and plush, the ormolu ornaments, and Turkey red carpets. "They give us plenty of shine and color as well as good measure in berth length," remarked the railroad tycoon approvingly.

The last three decades of the nineteenth century in Colorado west of the Ramparts, the men who built the railroads, the mines, and metals they exploited, the cities they built and abandoned, the tumults and the fanfares attendant upon vast and sudden riches, the pattern and color and pageantry of a human comedy, paralleled elsewhere but never quite

MIXED TRAIN FOR THE MILITARY

Probably, from its consist which includes a boxcar and six coaches followed by a caboose, a special military train or one carrying members of the C.C.C., this Rio Grande Southern makes a fine picture of ancient equipment functioning under modern conditions of war.

Lucius Beebe

DESTINY IN HUMBLE GUISE ON THE NARROW GAGE

Thrifty, hard-headed business men winced when the Federal Government advanced the Rio Grande Southern the sum of $65,000 to keep it a going concern. Nor did they see the light until a reeling world learned that many of the basic ores from which emerged the atom bomb were freighted out of southwestern Colorado by way of Durango and Montrose over the rusty rails of this financially shaky railroad which had been the dream of Otto Mears in the seventies. Although the photographer little guessed it at the time, here, behind a borrowed D. & R. G. W. engine near Vanadium in the lonely La Plata Mountains where there are no highways at all, is a train load of ores rich in radioactive elements bound for secret government plants. Two more narrow-gage locomotives are waiting at Placerville to boost the precious cargo over Dallas Divide to Ridgeway and the Ouray branch of the D. & R. G. W. The time is March, 1945.

THE DEEP SNOWS NEAR TIMBERLINE

Where, almost to timberline in Animas Canyon, the forest closes in on the narrow-gage tracks so that the evergreen boughs brush snow from the roofs of the high cars, the Denver & Rio Grande Western's every-other-day run from Durango to Silverton is ordered for the first time after the big blizzard of March, 1945. Save for the rotaries, the wedge plow shown here at the head end of a mixed consist with coach and caboose at the rear, is the most powerful snow-fighting equipment on the line. On the occasion of this run so great were the drifts in the desolate reaches of Animas Canyon that it required more than twenty hours for the train to cover fifty miles and the locomotive was forced twice to return over a large portion of the run for refueling and water. In these regions of Colorado a blizzard is not uncommon at any time of the year and old-timers remember, at the turn of the century, a Fourth of July baseball game which was called on account of snow. By the end of the third inning it was necessary to maintain a small fire to warm the second baseman and the game was called in the sixth when nine inches had fallen on the diamond and the spectators had sought shelter in Silverton's Palace Hotel bar.

OLD-TIME DOUBLE-HEADER

W. H. Jackson was not a railroad photographer so much as he was a specialist in Colorado scenery. Trains and trackage, however, frequently engage his incidental attentions as they were very much in the picture, both literally and figuratively, in his time. This double-header on the Denver & Rio Grande stopped to have its portrait recorded near Veta Pass on the now abandoned line near Ojo in the Sangre de Cristo Mountains. It is notable that while the baggage cars still are in the flat roof stage of development, the passenger cars of the period are already characterized by clerestory design for light and ventilation.

OVER THE CUMBRES IN NARROW-GAGE LUXURY

The Denver & Rio Grande Western's San Juan on the daily run between Durango and Alamosa in southwestern Colorado is the only narrow-gage name train with luxury equipment operating today in the United States. Its two minuscule lounge-observation-buffet cars, the Alamosa and Durango, are miniatures of conventional old-time Pullman parlor cars, complete with tiny kitchen, dining compartment, and railed-in sightseeing platform. Its schedule covers the two hundred miles between terminals entirely by daylight in each direction and it frequently crosses and recrosses the Colorado-New Mexico boundary and passes over the spectacular 10,000-foot Cumbres Pass in the San Juan Mountains as well as through the Toltec Gorge. Railroad amateurs as well as admirers of emphatically suburban scenery swear no railroad trip in the world equals its satisfactions and excitements.

Sanborn

THE GOOSE THAT GALLOPS ALONE

To operate one of the Rio Grande Southern's "Galloping Goose" railcars costs only fourteen cents a mile including repairs, fuel, and the operator's wages, and they have supplanted in recent years the road's traditional narrow-gage steam motive power and conventional coaches. Recently a "Galloping Goose," left momentarily unattended by its operator, coasted wildly down the east slope of Dallas Divide for a distance of fourteen miles and around a number of sharp reverse curves without jumping the track. No. 7 is shown here in the house track at Ridgeway, Colorado, where the Southern connects with the Montrose-Ouray line of the Denver & Rio Grande Western.

Lucius Beebe

TO PAGOSA, TO TOLTEC, TO ALAMOSA

The outside frame Mikado is pretty much standard motive power on Denver & Rio Grande Western narrow-gage freight hauls. In spite of their low drivers, heavy counter-balances, and seemingly complicated rod assemblies they wheel the little drags over amazing grades at a twenty-five or thirty miles clip, usually double-headed for mountain divisions. Running south out of Durango near Griffith on the way to the Cumbres Pass and Antonito with twenty-three cars, this team in tandem shows bravely against a background of Colorado winter.

R. H. Kindig

Otto C. Perry

MIXED MOTIVE POWER IN THE MOUNTAINS

Many of the locomotives of the picturesque and inaccessible Rio Grande Southern, Colorado's last but one surviving narrow-gage pike, are borrowed from the Denver & Rio Grande Western, the vast and affluent railroad which holds most of the Southern's paper. With a R. G. S. helper and D. & R. G. W. road engine this heavy freight is rolling down the La Plata Mountains between Dolores and Durango as the head brakeman looks over his consist to see that all is well.

IN THE FLOWERING OF THE LITTLE TRAINS

On the opposite page are shown (above) the Colorado and Southern's narrow-gage No. 70 with eight high cars crossing Clear Creek near the Stanley Mines a few miles west of Idaho Springs in 1938, and (below) a trainload of stock cars with cattle from the high ranges being hustled to market by the Denver and Rio Grande Western's No. 317 near Sapinero, Colorado.

duplicated on earth, are all now a part of the record and the legend. As in other golcondas and bonanzas in the American West, in Sutter's Creek, at Virginia City, in the Klondyke, and in the latter-day oil fields of Oklahoma and east Texas, the legend and the record are actually one, and brave and mighty things which in other chapters of the world's history would be ascribed to the romancing of ballad singers, minstrels, and newspaper reporters are imperishably engrossed in the factual chronicle. To draw the long bow in reporting contemporay life and the men who peopled it at Leadville in the seventies, say, would be beyond the imaginative capacities of the most alcoholic word artists in plug hats who came from the editorial rooms of James Gordon Bennett's New York *Herald* to gawk at specimens from the Little Pittsburgh and clap glad hands when Tom Walsh, owner of the Grand Hotel and partner with King Leopold of the Belgians in the Camp Bird Mine, opened champagne in gratifying and seemingly illimitable Niagaras. More sophisticated reporters in evening tailcoats in more modern surroundings have been known to clap hands at Friendship in Washington when Tom's daughter, Evalyn Walsh McLean, opened champagne in 1945 paid for out of the same veins of quartz.

In its early stages of development to Leadville, the firemen of the South Park had standing orders to keep their engines fired day and night at all times except when backshopping was actually necessary, as the possibility of Indian massacre was not yet a negligible consideration. The advertisements of Barlow and Sanderson's stage coach into town from Denver blandly assured prospective patrons: "Have no least apprehension of chance shots from Indians. We have shutters of iron and pistols are supplied ladies and gentlemen on request." Haw Tabor's Matchless Mine was only one of many a carbonate fairy tale with a happy ending: there were six prospering banks in Leadville at a time, fabulous characters like John Campion, Haw Tabor, Jack Morrisey and Alva Adams strode the streets in elegantly cut morning coats and financial-looking hats and their Colt's Patent Peacemakers clattered against the mahogany bar of the Saddle Rock as they marked the acquisition of another hundred-million-dollar property with tumblers of Monongahela and magnums of Louis Roederer, vintage of 1865! Was it any wonder that Jay

Gould, never entirely unimpressed by tangible evidences of enduring assets, should clap possessive eyes on the South Park, only eventually to have it fall into the embracing clutches of the Union Pacific! Those were the happy, blue-sky days!

Another community which bulked large in the railroading cycle of the times was Central City, today a well-upholstered and lovingly nourished ghost town and in the seventies a roaring gold and silver premises which, like all western communities of sudden and astounding affluence, made courtly overtures to the muses in a midst characterized by the most fragile gilt French furniture, the most genteel antimacassars, and the biggest brass spittoons that could be hauled up by mule team over the Canyon Trail from Idaho Springs.

The first narrow-gage railroad in the territory was built as the Colorado Central and was controlled by the Union Pacific. It was completed from Golden to Black Hawk, one mile below Central City, in 1872 and to Georgetown in 1876, and when it was put through to Central its track ran a distance of four miles to make the ascent from Black Hawk of something slightly under five hundred feet. Distance in those days, when measured in terms of elevation, meant nothing.

Uncle Horace Greeley, as has been previously noted, was particularly impressed by Central, and if the menu for New Year's Day dinner at the Teller House more than a decade after he had breasted the ten per cent grade of Eureka Street is any sample, Central was a town that did itself proud, gastronomically speaking at least. The bill of fare which ushered the miners into the year 1873 included ten entrees, fifteen vegetables, eight "cold ornamented dishes," fifteen roasts and a score of game dishes, including blue wing duck, mountain grouse, saddle of antelope with clove sauce, stuffed wild turkey, haunch of venison, Rocky Mountain black bear with currant jelly, prairie chicken with drip gravy, hump of buffalo calf, and mallard duck with apples. As a climax to this modest collation was served, to the wonderment and delight of guests, "The Teller House In Sugar, Illuminated With Central Gas." Obviously Peter Delmonico in New York had never done anything as enterprisingly esthetic as this, and S. E. Bush, proprietor of the Teller, received the congratulations of the community with the batted eyes and modesty of mien characteristic in later years of Nobel Prize winners and exhibitors of winning steers at the beef shows in Denver.

The rails of the Colorado and Southern, which inherited the Colorado Central, to Black Hawk and Central, were only torn up in 1941, and a private Palace car, rescued from the unhappy destruction, is to this day concealed among the out-buildings of a wealthy Denver fancier of antiquities of the storied past.

A major tumult, or rather series of scuffles which attended Colorado's early railroad-building days was the prolonged encounter between its two major transport systems, the Santa Fe and the Rio Grande, for trackage rights and control of the passes of the Raton and Glorieta into New Mexico and the Royal Gorge, gateway to the riches of recently opened Leadville mines and the center plateaus of the territory behind the Rampart Range. The Rio Grande, under the direction of General Palmer, had started south from Denver in 1871, bound for El Paso and, eventually, Mexico City. It was a three-foot-gage experiment, based on General Palmer's observation of similar operations in Europe, and from the outset was moderately successful in exploiting Colorado resources in the plains and foothills of the Rockies.

The discovery of gold and silver in Leadville in the early seventies, however, made it obvious to both the Rio Grande and the Santa Fe, then progressing westward under the direction of President Thomas Nickerson and his directorate of Boston bankers (for at this time, as in the early years of the financing of the Union Pacific, the greatest banks of issue and underwriting were still located in State Street), that the future of Colorado railroading lay in traversing the mountains rather than skirting them. At the same time President Nickerson realized that if the Santa Fe were ever to achieve anything beyond the Atchison and Topeka of its original incorporated name, it would have to beat Palmer's narrow-gage track gangs over the passes into New Mexico.

The warfare for the control of these two vital passages never achieved the status of a war of lethal gunfire and bloodshed. With commendable celerity and a great deal of hard breathing and swearing, the construction gangs of the Santa Fe first got a shovel-hold in the Raton and retained it through all the courts which had jurisdiction in the matter.

In the Royal Gorge dispute things were of a slightly more colorful order and the profanity was reported to have achieved a level which would have been regarded with favor even by the legendary military in Flanders. Also the dispute raged through the courts for the better part of a decade and the single line of track that it was possible to lay through the Canyon itself was several times and alternately dominated by the rival railroads and their private armies. Most of the weapons employed were sheriffs' writs, but at Pueblo, toward the final stages of the game, the Santa Fe engaged the services of Bat Masterson, the famous Dodge City peace officer who swore a very great oath indeed to shoot General Palmer's men as soon as they might show on the horizon. Witnesses later deposed that profanity had never before achieved such heights of imagination, resourcefulness and vehemence west of the Mississippi.

In the end, however, in a flurry of opinions, precedents, and genealogical exchanges between the interested parties, the Rio Grande won the final legal round and a treaty of peace was signed in faraway Boston with suitable decantings of Flying Cloud Madeira and S. S. Pierce's best bottlings of Lawrence's Medford Rum, a spirits which surprised and gladdened the Denver bankers who had innocently imagined Uncle Dick Wooten's Taos Lightning to be the ultimate distillation of concentrated essence of hellebore.

Three-quarters of a century after the first traffic started rolling over the Denver and Pacific the wheel had come full circle. Many a brave little railroad which came into expansive being in the fabulous seventies and eighties is now with history, existing only in the files of the *Rocky Mountain News* with, perhaps, vestigial traces of its once busy roadbed discernible to the instructed eye in the cuts of some scenic highway.

Scarcely more than a dozen railroads are today in main-line operation in the Centennial State, where in 1912 there were a total of sixty, but even this modest tale, compared to the top-heavy tally of carriers of fifty-odd years ago, furnishes some of the brightest and most dramatic pages in the Official Guide. Gone are the Florence and Cripple Creek, the Gilpin County Trams, the narrow-gage divisions of the Colorado and Southern; gone, too, is the Silverton and Northern, its little varnish cars translated into lunch wagons along the Million Dollar Highway,

Lucius Beebe

THE SANTA FE'S EL CAPITAN IN RATON PASS

"THE WOLF THAT FOLLOWS, THE FAWN THAT FLIES"

"Atalanta In Calydon"

Dramatic and unaccustomed is the teaming of this graceful, high-wheeled Pacific passenger engine with a grumbling, powerful Mallet on the head end of a long Union Pacific freight drag heading east on the long grade out of Laramie, Wyoming. The probable explanation is that a great deal of U. P. backshop work is done at Cheyenne and that, although it can hardly be of material assistance in its capacity of lead engine, the Pacific has been coupled to the pilot of the conventional freight hog to save being dispatched as a light engine to the Cheyenne shops.

Lucius Beebe

THE MALLET AND THE MILITARY

The huge, low-pressure front cylinders which are the hallmark of the true Mallet or articulated compound locomotive are abundantly visible in this photograph showing a Denver & Rio Grande Western troop train, double-headed, thundering through a cut in the main line west out of Denver at Leyden, Colorado. These Mallets are peculiarly adapted to the grades and tunnels which abound in the fifty-mile east approach to the Moffat because of their vast drawbar pull and flexibility on sharp curves.

DAILY OUT OF DENVER

Every morning at 9:50 this stylish little varnish, No. 1 of the Denver & Salt Lake, sometime with two cars, sometime with three, sets out from the D. & S. L. depot in Denver for Craig, 230 miles upstate, behind a high-stepping ten-wheeler brave with polish and a large brass number plate on its smokebox. Here it is rolling along between the north portal of Tunnel No. 1 at Coal Creek and the station at Plainview, Colorado.

C. M. Clegg

"AND DUST AND HURRYING HORSEMEN; LO THEIR CHIEF"

"Atalanta In Calydon"

The thundering exhausts of six pairs of high-pressure cylinders and low ascend to heaven as the Atchison, Topeka & Santa Fe's The Chief surges up the steep grades of the Raton Pass at Wootton, Colorado. The helper is a ponderous Mallet which lends a hand from Trinidad as far as Raton while the road engine, one of the Santa Fe's fleet-footed Northerns, is at the head end from La Junta all the way to Los Angeles. C. M. Clegg obtained this stunningly dramatic action shot with a Kodak Medalist opened to f 6.5 at 1/400 second with Kodak Super XX film. The Mallet running on the head as helper, No. 1794, was formerly Norfolk and Western No. 2014.

DIESEL ON THE DIVIDE

The D. & R. G. W. on its Denver-Salt Lake freight runs has heavily committed itself to Diesel-electric motive power supplied by such 5400 horsepower quadruple units as this shown at the traditionally smoky end of seventy cars of wartime freight at the west approach to Tunnel No. 1 on the Denver side of the Moffat. Even such potent head-end power as this, however, isn't alone sufficient for the two per cent grades and fifty mile uphill climb of the east ramparts of the Rockies, and at the other end, or cut into the middle of the train, there is invariably one of the road's tremendous Mallets.

Lucius Beebe

SUPER DE LUXE SUPER POWER: THE SUPER CHIEF

Lucius Beebe

THE ROCKY MOUNTAIN ROCKET

Three daily streamlined Diesel-electric luxury trains run in each direction between Chicago and Denver as well as numerous conventional steam-powered passenger hauls. They are the Union Pacific's City of Denver, the Burlington's Denver Zephyr and, shown here, the Rock Island's Rocky Mountain Rocket which approaches the Queen City over the U. P. iron from Limon. The Rock Island's own main line runs south at Limon, running into the celebrated resort city of Colorado Springs.

Lucius Beebe

HOW TO SEE COLORADO IN COMFORT

Near Salida, where the right-of-way of the D. & R. G. W. parallels the Arkansas River through grim and forbidding canyons, the Scenic Limited, train No. 1, between Denver and Salt Lake via the Royal Gorge Route, heads into the afternoon sun. Placer miners who set up their sluices and riffles and still pan gold are often visible hereabouts from its observation platform, survivors of the old times when the quest of gold in its rivers and hillsides was a stronger lure to Colorado than the coal mines and great cattle ranges are today.

FIRST NO. 5, THE EXPOSITION FLYER

Between Leyden, Colorado, and Tunnel No. 1 above Coal Creek on the east approach to the Moffat Tunnel the tracks of the Denver & Salt Lake describe an amazing series of convolutions to gain altitude in their attack upon the Ramparts of the Rockies. In a space of a few miles the iron describes three almost complete circles before it achieves the brief tangent between Tunnel No. 1 and Plainview. Here the Denver & Rio Grande Western, which has trackage rights over the D. & S. L. as far as Bond, sends its Exposition Flyer double-headed on the overnight run between Denver and Salt Lake with green flags flying to indicate the presence behind it of another section operating as Second No. 5.

C. M. Clegg

THE SANTA FE CHIEF, DOUBLE-HEADING IN THE RATON

"SINCE THEN ON MANY A CAR YOU'LL SEE
A BROOMSTICK, PLAIN AS PLAIN CAN BE!"

Oliver Wendell Holmes

Between Golden, once almost the principal city of Colorado Territory, and Leyden, where profitable coal mines are operated to this day, and Denver runs the standard-gage Denver and Intermountain Railroad over fifty-three miles of its own and leased freight trackage. Its little electric engines with their overhead trolleys which so captivated the fancy of Dr. Holmes that they were forever after known in New England as "broomstick cars" and the line's own cabooses are familiar sights along the meadows which bound the main highway west into the mountains. It is, of course, the utilitarian antithesis of the elegantly appointed "Electroliners" of the Chicago, North Shore and Milwaukee, which boast buffets and dining cars, stand-up bars, modernist decor, and eighty-mile-an-hour carding through the rich cities of western Lake Michigan.

THIS SILVER STREAK IS THE TEXAS ZEPHYR

Daily between Denver and Colorado Springs, Trinidad, Fort Worth, and Dallas over the iron of the Colorado and Southern and the old Fort Worth and Denver City flash the Burlington's Texas Zephyrs behind 4,000-horsepower Diesel-electric engines. Their consist includes head-end revenue cars, reclining seat coaches, diners, and streamlined Pullmans. This Zephyr, southbound, was snapped near Walsenburg.

WESTBOUND, THE EXPOSITION FLYER

Upper left:
Lucius Beebe

The Denver & Rio Grande Western's No. 5 with a powerful, low-wheeled Mountain type locomotive as helper ahead of the regular road engine, makes a handsome picture of mountain railroading as it heads west with ten cars out of Chicago bound for San Francisco at Leyden, Colorado.

SUMMER EVENING PASTORAL

Lower left:
C. M. Clegg

Although to the exacting voyager this little Colorado and Southern passenger train rolling up to Denver from Texas may not be in a class with the Burlington's gleaming Texas Zephyr, its mixed consist, with a car of perishable freight, post office and mail storage cars, coaches, a diner and a lone Pullman, makes a summer evening pastoral as it climbs a short grade on the single track at Holloway, Colorado. Its power is a C. & S. high-wheel Pacific with the Burlington herald on its tender and characteristic feed water heater at the top of the smokebox.

THIS IS BIG-TIME RAILROADING

More than any other name in railroading, the words Union Pacific quicken the pulse and lay hold upon the imagination. The surge of its traffic across the reaches of a continent is as implacable and relentless as the tides; its name is strong medicine in counting house and signal tower. There was no western land before the U. P. came and for three-quarters of a century it has been as much a part of the American scheme of things as the secret ballot, the trotting horse, and Congress gaiters. Here is a mile-long freight with a Mike as helper and one of the 3900 series articulated road engines coming up the grade a few miles south of Cheyenne on the Denver run.

WHEELING THE C. & S. TONNAGE

Over the entire depth of Colorado from Wyoming to New Mexico and in the shadow all the way of the mountain ranges which bisect the state on a north and south axis, the Colorado and Southern Railroad, owned and controlled by the Burlington Lines, maintains its main line with frequent feeders and branches. Its greatest revenue derives from the coal and mineral ores, stock and farm produce of this fabulously affluent commonwealth. This powerful C. & S. Santa Fe (2-10-2) locomotive is heading southward near Palmer Lake with a mile of mixed freight on the right-of-way over which it enjoys trackage rights with the Santa Fe and Denver & Rio Grande Western.

and vanished are the switchbacks, so celebrated in their day, of the Argentine Central on the mountainsides of Silver Plume. In their stead there vibrates the crescendo snore of the Rio Grande's Diesel-electric units on the Salt Lake freight haul, there flashes the silver of the streamliners of the Burlington and there echo the thunderous exhausts of the Santa Fe's double- and tripled-shotted road engines and helpers climbing out of Trinidad into the ravines of the Raton. Colorado railroading has become very bigtime indeed, even its remaining short lines being held in fief by the mighty Colorado Iron and Fuel Company or as feeders to the transcontinental Union Pacific, but the lift and the excitements that must always be associated with mountain railroading are still abundant.

A glance at the railroad map of Colorado shows, as might be expected, an almost geometrical pattern of main lines from the east crossing each other in symmetric figures and separating again at such approximately equidistant division points as Sterling, Limon, and La Junta, to reconverge upon Greeley, Denver, Colorado Springs, Pueblo, and Trinidad. The roads participating in this tolerably simple geographic saraband are, of course, the Union Pacific, Burlington, Rock Island, and Santa Fe. Beyond the barrier of the Rampart Range the mountain passes are threaded in a generally westerly direction by the Rio Grande in three places—Denver, Pueblo, and Walsenburg—and by the dramatic mountain iron of the Santa Fe in the Raton on the Colorado–New Mexico border. At intermediate points there are minor skirmishes between the mountains and the Mikados of such lines as the Colorado and Southern, the Denver & Salt Lake, the Midland Terminal, the Colorado Railroad, and the Colorado & Wyoming. Most of these tap for their various operators the coal resources of their immediate locale, and their most notable member is the Denver and Salt Lake running over the Moffat between Denver and Bond and Craig. The only two great systems, however, to essay the Continental Divide and achieve over its altitudes a terminus in the western land are the Rio Grande and the Santa Fe.

Of all the little lines in Colorado and, indeed, in the United States, the non-rail-minded voyager is probably most familiar with the Manitou and Pike's Peak, the rack-and-pinion railroad which reaches nine miles from Manitou Springs, near Colorado Springs, to the summit of the hurricane-swept mountain which in winter dominates the whole of Colorado with its majestic and terrifying beard of driven snow. In 1884 a project was started for a Pike's Peak line with three-foot track, adhesion power, and a developed length of thirty miles to limit the ruling grade of five per cent. Traces of this project in the form of undeveloped grades can still be discerned in Crystal Park, but the scheme was abandoned and it was not until 1890 that the present road with an average grade of sixteen per cent and a maximum of twenty-five, ascends to a level of 14,000 feet above the sea. In its entire stretch there are no trestles and only four short plate girder bridges.

Less familiar to the public, but possessed of even more charms for the connoisseur of railroading are such little pikes as the Laramie, North Park & Western, the Great Western, the Midland Terminal, the Colorado & Wyoming, and the Colorado & South-Eastern.

The Laramie, North Park & Western, a cattle, oil, and produce feeder to the Union Pacific at Laramie, Wyoming, but with most of its trackage in the desolate North Park and Snowy Range mountains of Colorado, is a picturesque single track with a train daily in alternate directions between its terminal and Coalmont, by way of Walden, Colorado. Passenger service is available in its roomy but highly informal cabooses and grosses the road about $30 a month through the year. Possessed of a handful of low-wheeled Mikados with spark arresters of startling design, the road's daily run of 110 miles is an all-day proposition, but its traffic is sufficient to warrant in a single recent year the replacement alone of 55,000 ties at a cost of approximately $1.25 a tie, which will serve as an index to the store set by it by its mighty parent company. The rich ranch lands which adjoin its rambling right-of-way, the dense fir forest of the Snowy Mountains, and the recent opening of not inconsiderable oil wells near Windmill Hollow more than warrant the continued existence of the railroad.

Farther downstate the Great Western Railroad, a property of the Great Western Sugar Company, maintains a surprisingly complex minor net work of operations and trackage between its terminal town of Loveland and Longmont, Officer, Milliken, Johnstown, Windsor, and Eaton. Although it no longer maintains passenger service and its last combina-

FOR A MOUNTAIN RUN: THE MOUNTAINEER

The daily overnight run between Denver and Montrose, Colorado, on the stand-ard-gage iron of the D. & R. G. W. by way of the Moffat Tunnel and Grand Junction is made by a sleek little coach and Pullman flyer called the Mountaineer. Assigned to the run are a pair of trim ten-wheelers of speedy design with more attention to paint and polish than most engines get. Here is one of them clipping off a good sixty a few miles north of Montrose.

tion coach reposes in a state of genteel decline in the Loveland yards, the Great Western is a common carrier, and high cars from the Central of Georgia, Central Vermont, Southern Pacific, and Pennsylvania are as familiar sights in its daily scheduled time freights as its own hopper cars.

The main-line outlets of the Great Western are the Colorado and Southern and Union Pacific, and its nine locomotives on the active roster gleam with the high polish which only private ownership and pride of management can, seemingly, achieve. The G. W. lists two switchers of 0-6-0 type with drawbar pull of 31,000 pounds, six Consolidations with drawbar pull of up to 34,000 pounds and one Decapod, the pride of the backshops, with a drawbar pull of 45,000 pounds. At active seasons, when the beet sugar harvest is moving, all nine engines are in daily operation and the road hauls annually something in excess of 13,500 carloads of grain, coal, hay, live stock, canned milk, and similar produce.

In the remaining trackage of the Midland Terminal, extending from its rambling yards and shops a few miles west of the Rio Grande's depot, shared with the Rock Island, at Colorado Springs, to the loops, sidings and switchbacks of Victor and the weed-grown house tracks of Cripple Creek, are the traces of the once mightily ambitious Colorado Midland. The Colorado Midland, a standard-gage road, was built in the middle eighties to shortcut the narrow-gage line of the Rio Grande, and it and the later Colorado Springs and Cripple Creek served this romantic territory when it was in its golden noontide of wealth and promise.

At one time the Colorado Midland and the Rio Grande together operated a joint project between Newcastle and Grand Junction for a connection with the Rio Grande Western (now D. & R. G. W.), and the high point in its history was the building of its startling series of loops over Hagerman Pass. At the time of its dissolution at the hands of the courts, the Colorado Midland represented the largest railroad abandonment in the world, but the trains of the Midland Terminal still do a very considerable daily business, sometimes powered by as many as five and six engines to a train, hauling empty ore cars up to Victor and braking them down again over the steep grades at Midland and Divide.

In the southern region of Colorado are four little railroads still in active operation which engage the attention of historians, although the casual traveler may well be unaware of their existence. At Blanca, on its Walsenburg–Alamosa run, the D. & R. G. W. meets the daily in-and-out train from Questa of the San Luis Valley Southern, an agricultural railroad in San Luis Park. At Monte Vista the single surviving locomotive of the San Luis Central shifts cars on the D. & R. G. W.'s exchange tracks, mostly potato hauls in the proper season, and the Colorado & South-Eastern, a coal-haul railroad with its origins in the haunted coal shafts of Delagua and Ludlow, rolls thirty or forty cars of coal down the grade of the Colorado and Southern every morning into Trinidad. Every afternoon it consumes three times the time to haul them back again up the grade and empty behind its one remaining teakettle, a Mogul of dateless origin and doubtless dusty destinies, once the lean pockets it serves have produced the final carloading of low-grade fuel.

Running into the smoky valley which shelters Trinidad, too, is a somewhat less sooty and more distinguished little road, the Colorado & Wyoming, notable for its three separate and nonconnecting divisions, the Southern between Trinidad and Tercio, the Middle and entirely invisible trackage within the industrial foundry-fortress of the Colorado Fuel and Iron Company at Pueblo, and the Northern Division operating only in the State of Wyoming. The little roundhouse and shops of the Southern Division at Segundo, where every lathe and hoist chain could stand inspection with glacé kid gloves without soiling, is a model among rail installations, and the twin Consolidations which alternate in active service and in the rear shops of this gleaming and meticulous railroad are paradigms of spit and polish and perfection of grooming.

To the railroad historian, whose sensibilites must be attuned to the past even as his attention is geared to the present, no aspect of Colorado railroading is possessed of so much charm and fascination as its remaining narrow-gage trackage. There is, in truth, in the three-foot rails of the Denver & Rio Grande Western and the Rio Grande Southern, little enough active and operating narrow-gage, but over them hangs the wistful narrow-gage past and they are implicit with souvenirs and memories of all the little railroads of other times—the Florence and Cripple Creek, the Denver, Utah and Pacific, the Silverton Northern, the Denver, Boulder and Western, the Crystal River and San Juan, the Argentine Central. In the exhausts thudding over Marshall Pass there are echoes of sparkling railroad yesterdays and in the beautiful "San Juan," the last luxury narrow-gage passenger train in America, are happy vestiges of all the little varnish trains that have vanished forever from the tracks.

On the wilderness stretches of the track of the Rio Grande Southern, the 162-mile main line of which connects towns a scant sixty miles apart by air line, only freight is now dispatched behind steam motive power, and often enough its helper engines bear the lettering of the D. & R. G. W., its parent company and holder of its entire bonded indebtedness. The road's old-time car herald with the legend "Silver San Juan Scenic Line" has long since disappeared and with it the steam-powered passenger locals which once served 4,000 square miles of sparsely populated territory in southwestern Colorado. In their place have appeared gasoline-powered motor-coach-freight vehicles locally known as "Galloping Geese," a compromise with more conventional railroading which probably saved from complete oblivion the romantic road which reaches from Durango west and north to Dolores and through the storied San Miguel Mountains to Rico, Lizard Head, Ophir, Telluride, and Placerville.

The narrow-gage division of the Denver & Rio Grande Western, however, presents a different and more prosperous aspect of mountain railroading. Durango—a dusty town of excellent two-bit bourbon, thick steaks, Chinamen of substantial commerce, and Indians in red Saturday night blankets to their ankles and in conditions indicative of powerful alcoholic endeavor—is probably the narrow-gage capital of the world. Here the three divisions of the D. & R. G. W.'s narrow-gage universe converge from Silverton on the north, Farmington on the south, and Alamosa two-hundred-odd miles to the east. And every other day freights arrive and depart on the Rio Grande Southern for Dolores and the north. There is a daily luxury passenger train, the "San Juan," whose morning departure and afternoon arrival from Alamosa with mail and papers and passengers from Denver is the event of the day, and over the same route there are daily freight drags with the accustomed double-headed power of the Rio Grande's powerful outside frame Mikados panting urgently back and forth across the Colorado–New Mexico border and over the 10,000-foot summit of Cumbres Pass, where the snow drifts thirty feet deep in winter time and the wolves can still be heard howling when the wind sets right.

The D. & R. G. W.'s fabled Santa Fe–Antonito run was abandoned only a few years ago and the tracks from Pagosa to Pagosa Springs have long since been torn up, but at least once a week each way there is a narrow-gage freight between Alamosa and Salida where the longest narrow-gage tangent in the world stretches for fifty-three uninterrupted miles between Alamosa and Villagrove. The slim gage no longer operates between Montrose and Gunnison above the tortuous windings of the Gunnison River, but freight runs regularly between Gunnison and Salida over the Marshall Pass, and when the mines are operating, heavy ore trains roll ponderously down from Anthracite and Crested Butte to the extensive Gunnison yards. At Gunnison, also, is the largest narrow-gage roundhouse and shops in regular operation, and there are as many as twelve or fourteen diminutive engines, Mikados and switchers, some of them inherited veterans of the Crystal River and San Juan and the Florence and Cripple Creek, and at least one of them a standard-gage, heavy-duty Rio Grande ten-wheeler with an impressive tender cut down to size, dozing in the warm darkness or sleeping soundly with drawn fires through the mountain winters.

The narrow-gage railroads are, to the imaginative mind, repositories of all the wonder-freighted Colorado chronicle. Their diminutive trucks clattering ceaselessly over the perpetual rails recall the days when thirty-six railroad companies filed papers to build from Denver to Leadville alone and when former President Grant, in the gilt and ormolu precincts of the Clarendon Hotel in Leadville, pushed his top hat to the back of his head, accepted a scoop of forty-rod from Haw Tabor and began the Civil War all over again, commencing with John Brown in Kansas. They had their beginnings before ever John Morrisey unthriftily spent the millions from the Highland Mary in the Rue de la Paix to end in the Denver poorhouse, and they have survived to bury the great Spencer Penrose and see Evalyn Walsh MacLean, with the Hope Diamond around her neck above the Star of the East, the familiar friend of another rakehelly President in the White House. They were rolling their freight when Lord Dunraven was hoisting tall ones in the bar of the unbelievable Windsor in Denver with Lawrence Barrett and Richard Mansfield, and their Palace cars were gliding smoothly through Fairplay when Buffalo Bill was nervously eating cloves before being presented to Queen Victoria. They saw the beginnings of a countless tale of Colorado fortunes and families, dynasties, and lofty destinies, and they saw the decline and end of some.

Gene Fowler has remarked, as quoted elsewhere in this book: "The history of Greece was written in its monuments; that of America in its hotels." It does not seem to indulge too imaginative a fancy to say that much of the history of Colorado, at least its richest, its gustiest, and most enchanting, has been written in its narrow-gage railroads.

Right: Lucius Beebe

Lucius Beebe

6
CRUMMIES

IN THE gaudy lexicon of railroad jargon it has more names than any other property in the economy of the high iron, even more than there are for engines and engine drivers. It is caboose, crummy, way car, van, cage, doghouse, drone house, bouncer, bedhouse, buggy, chariot, shelter house, glory wagon, go-cart, hack, hut, monkey wagon, pavilion, palace, parlor, brainbox, zoo, diner, kitchen, perambulator, parlor, cabin car, and shanty. There are probably others in a variety only bounded by the limitations of human imagining and the vocabulary of profane and uninhibited men.

It is the freight crew's home away from home, a rolling microcosm of domesticity, a shelter against the blast, a premises as masculine in its implications as a corner saloon, a light to guide a man in the dark, the period and apostrophe at the end of the completed sentence of a train. To the perfectionist there can exist no symphony without a coda, no finished repast without the benediction of cognac. So to the railroad perfectionist there can be no train, in the technical sense and as an esthetic entity, distinguished from a cut of cars, without a caboose complete with markers. There are, shamefully enough in a degenerate age, transcontinental Pullman trains without observation cars. There are also pork chops without apple sauce. Either is more thinkable than a freight, whether redball manifest or modest local, effacing itself on passing tracks for every other train on the employees' card, without a crummy.

Probably there is more warmth of homeliness and sentiment about a hack at the end of a string of high cars, a little self-contained world of animation and reality as it diminishes down the tracks behind a hustling symbol freight, than exists for any other of a railroad's tangible properties. Neither the drowsing water tank in the desert nor the semaphore giving green in a cut in the high hills nor even the glitter and crisp linen and fresh cut flowers of the de luxe dining-car are possessed of quite the qualities to captivate the imagining that belong to the red-painted caboose with a wisp of smoke from its disreputable chimney pot, canted at a rakish angle and secured against complete disintegration by a length of rusty baling wire.

Because of its unique status in the roster of railroad equipment, too, the caboose achieves an individuality unshared by rolling stock in any other category, freight or passenger. Because, unlike all sorts of freight and some passenger cars, a crummy seldom rides any rails but those of its home company, it is not subject to the qualifying regulations which govern the design and maintenance of stock cars, reefers, or tanks which must operate over a vast multiplicity of different systems. It is an individualist, a maverick, proud of its own eccentricities of character and disdainful, in its usually shabby raffishness, of the well-bred uniformity of Pullmans and high cars alike. The caboose is the Bohemian of railroad rolling stock society.

For this reason it is possible to find on some roads, such, for example, as the Boston and Maine and Lehigh Valley, crummies equipped with the last word in high-speed passenger trucks and all steel construction, while on other systems there are still in service cabooses with wooden underframes which, when a pusher is used on grades, require that the engine be cut in between the hack and the last revenue car equipped, according to I.C.C. regulations, with steel frames.

Because of its comparatively humble function and utilitarian design, the history of the evolution of the caboose is largely a matter of conjecture. Unlike the proud designers of McKay and Aldus, Breese, Kneeland and Company, Hinckley and Drury, and other builders who left specifications and architect's elevations of their every locomotive for the wonderment and imitation of posterity, there was no William Mason of the crummies to leave his imprimatur on the hacks that came into emergent being in the sixties and seventies to roll across the western lands or through the woodlands of the Deep South. The caboose came into being conditioned by the imaginings and necessites of finger-shy link and pin brakemen and chin-whiskered freight conductors who required a shelter from the storm in which to light their ponderous globular lanterns and tally their way-bills, and who begged or stole a disused high car or rigged a precarious pavilion on a flat to serve their purpose.

Probably the first cabooses were much of a pattern with the shelter cars still current on the Terminal Railroad of St. Louis trains, a sort of rough-hewn gazebo erected and stayed in the middle of a flatcar. Or they may have been a simple boxcar with windows sawed to suit and a cannonball stove installed in a sandbox in the corner. Presumably they were side door crummies, without benefit of end doors and platforms, for the side door hack has only recently been more or less universally outlawed. Certainly the earliest of the tribe boasted no raised cupola or clerestory window, an innovation which may have been the invention of some Christopher Wren of the Illinois Central or a Bullfinch of the Camden and Amboy. Properly speaking the Bullfinch or bay window hack is a very modern institution indeed and is standard practice only known to a handful of roads such as the Baltimore and Ohio and Milwaukee, which have found that a bulge on the side of a car is less conducive to falls and injuries to personnel than a perch on a vantage point poked through the roof.

Going to the other extreme, there are the crummies of the Rock Island which obviate all shelter whatsoever and provide the train crew with a sort of fore-and-aft love seat attached crosswise in the center of the roof, open to the elements and facing in both directions.

Probably the first refinement to appear on the converted boxcar caboose, the side door entry to which caused the loss of so many lives as to be one of the classic menaces of railroading along with the lethal car stove and the pre-Janney coupling devices, was a simple one in the form of a curved grabiron which, it was discovered, helped swing a know-how brakeman up the step of a moving string of cars. The most modern innovations include solid steel construction, chromium trim on inside furniture, sponge rubber mattresses, stainless steel cooking facilities, built-in iceboxes, individual clothes lockers and, on certain divisions of the Pennsylvania, caboose-to-engine telephone connections by short-wave radio intercommunication.

The word caboose in a variety of more or less germaine meanings has been a part of several languages since it first appeared as *cambose* or *camboose* in the records of the French navy in the middle of the eighteenth century. Its initial appearance in English literature, according

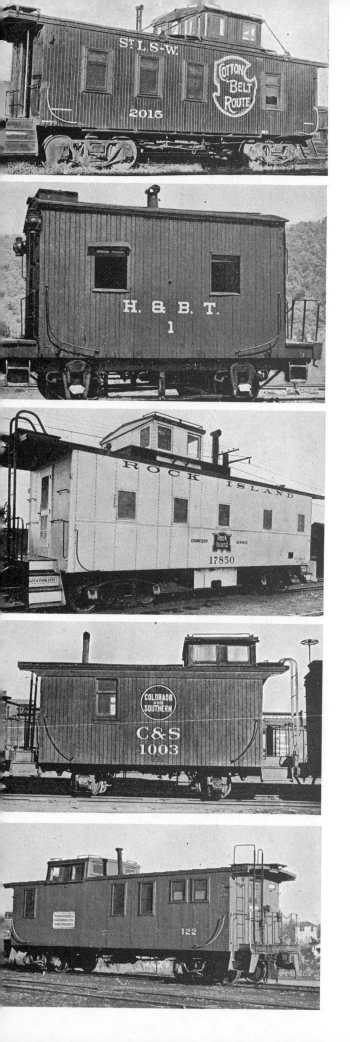

This Cotton Belt crummie, photographed by C. W. Witbeck at Shreveport, Louisiana, displays the road's car herald big and bold for all the world to see.

The Hampton & Branchville's caboose No. 1 boasts neither clerestory nor bay window in its architectural economy. Photographed by C. I. Collom.

This stylish Rock Island all-steel car is coated with aluminum paint, making it ten per cent cooler in summer, and has built-in bunks and other modernities for night crews. Railroad Magazine photograph.

Once this Colorado and Southern narrow-gage caboose rolled over the historic right-of-way up Clear Creek to Black Hawk and Idaho Springs in Colorado's lusty youth. F. D. Kelley photograph, courtesy of Railroad Magazine.

The Midland Valley's No. 122 also bears the legend of its allied roads, the Oklahoma City–Ada–Atoka and the Kansas, Oklahoma & Gulf. Photographed at Denison, Texas, by C. M. Clegg.

The characteristic black way car of the Denver & Rio Grande Western has white painted steps and rails for safety at night and unusual four-paned windows in its cupola. Railroad Magazine photograph.

The trucks of this Pickering Lumber Company caboose, caught by Gerald Best at Standard, California, appear large and substantial enough for service on a car twice its size.

Side door crummies like this ancient Atchison, Topeka & Santa Fe hack are outlawed in Kansas, but still see service in Oklahoma and the Texas Panhandle. Photograph by Preston George.

Possessed of a peculiar fascination for railroaders are such tiny and intimate cabooses as this neatly appointed No. 5 of the Raritan River, snapped on a New Jersey siding by C. M. Clegg.

These smartly designed and handsomely painted Cumberland and Pennsylvania, now Western Maryland, cars displayed the railroad's heralds on their platforms and constituted a rolling advertisement for the company. S. P. Davidson photograph.

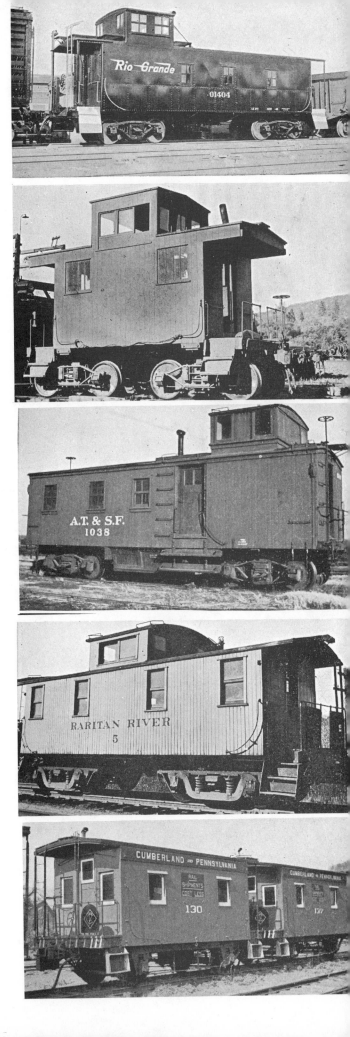

HAPPY VALLEY EQUIPMENT

The Lehigh is pleased to designate these super-de-luxe crummies as "cabin cars" in its releases for the general public. No matter what its name, however, the Taj Mahal of cabooses pictured above includes in the roster of its installations built-in ice water coolers, a refrigerator, sponge rubber bunk cushions, individual lockers for members of the train crew, enamel wash sink, and a cream and black stream-lined paint job. About the only vestigial traces of the old-time way car which survive are the cast-iron car stove with its sheet-iron pipe leading through the roof and the coal-oil lamps secured to the walls above the conductor's desk, neither of which are visible in this picture. Only the Happy Valley, where good railroaders go when they die, and the Lehigh Valley could dream up such a luxury hack.

to the New English Dictionary, was when in 1805 in the record of a New England shipwreck the New York *Chronicle* reported that a member of the crew, "William Duncan, drifted aboard the canboose." In 1859 the word caboose, spelled as it is today and used in a railroading context, appeared in the litigation attendant upon a lawsuit against the New York and Harlem Railway, and Bill Knapke reports that in the same year a traveler visiting a New England town was struck by the sight of a flat car on which there was a sort of shelter or pavilion, and subsequently wrote: "The men had erected a caboose in which to cook their meals."

The next recorded literary appearance of such a structure probably had reference to something other than a mobile shack, for in 1883, the *Century Magazine* described a fête champêtre at which "the lawn was studded with cabooses." The same year the Chicago *Times* chronicles a news dispatch including reference to "the caboose of the construction train containing several men and boys." Its latest example, dated 1884, the New English Dictionary merely attributes to a "Dakota newspaper" and describes "four cars and a caboose running down the track," so that after that it may be taken as sufficiently current usage not to attract the attention of historians of the vernacular. The caboose was running down the track with sufficient momentum to carry it right down to the immediate, twentieth-century present.

While the literary origins of the caboose have been chronicled with such "on schedule" exactitude by the learned lexicographer, its factual genesis is somewhat more open to the whims and distortions of legend. Bill Knapke, however, who writes for *Railroad Magazine,* and who is also a gold mine of caboose lore, is willing to be reasonably exact in the matter of the beginnings of the institutional cupola which, for eighty-odd years, was the hallmark of the way car.

It was in the summer of 1863 that Conductor T. B. Watson of the very English Chicago and North Western was assigned to regular freight runs between Cedar Rapids and Clinton, Iowa, according to Mr. Knapke. His regular shack was being shopped and he was temporarily the unhappy captain of a somewhat disreputable boxcar which had, in some manner, come by a large circular hole in the roof. Shamed by his makeshift buggy and being something of a card or character, Watson determined to make the best of things and decided that comedy was indicated. As his consist clattered over the sixty-pound switch points into the Clinton yards, other trainmen and loiterers were fascinated to observe Watson's portly person, obviously supported by a requisitioned chair or packing case, protruding from the unseemly aperture while the fellow raised his hat and made courtly bows to all and sundry. In the course of his little act, however, Watson discovered that a clearance of a couple of feet above the roof of his car was an ideal vantage point from which to con the progress of his train, and he forthwith persuaded the road's master mechanic to enclose the position with glass against the weather and install a permanent deck underneath this clerestory. Thus the cupola was born.

The parallel between the caboose of railroad operations and the original and antecedent cook shack on the deck of a sailing ship is in no way merely one of etymology. Their exterior resemblance was obvious from the beginning and consideration of their function further heightens the resemblance. Both are designed as strictly functional parts in the integrated economy of travel. Both are made to withstand the assaults of nature upon man's inherent frailties, to stay and comfort him when the rains descend and great winds blow upon the earth. Both are destined to voyage into far places and see strange and wonderful things, and each of them nourishes and strengthens a breed of men at once individualistic and disciplined beyond the ordinary run. And, of course, the ship's galley and the little red caboose are both dedicated, primarily, to that great equalizer and most common of all human common denominators: food!

A great deal has been written and sung on the subject of way-car food, and it is probable that the legend increases in the telling, since the facilities of even the most elaborately commissioned shack can scarcely live up to the requirements, say, of a Scotto or Escoffier. But under unusual and peculiarly characteristic circumstances, even the simplest fare has been known to assume a certain charm, and the saga of caboose cooking would never have been as firmly established if it had not exercised, for the men interested in its consumption, a considerable persuasiveness. The baked beans and bread puddings, the pork chops and pan-fried potatoes, and the illimitable varieties of hot breads evolved by generations of chariot chefs sustained many and many a famished brakeman and conductor on desert divisions before the days of Harvey Houses and in times when it was not uncommon to tie up for rest on the road miles from the nearest eating place. Then, too, old-timers can recall forgotten runs on Down East pikes and even on the great trunk lines of Canada where the train crew found it handy to take along a sporting rifle in the interest of venison and the engineer was known to have to make repairs with singular regularity adjacent to favored trout streams. Rule G is more widely and respectfully observed, in all probability, than any similar regulation on the subject of alcohol anywhere in the world, but that crummy ice boxes occasionally carry a consignment of the best Milwaukee or St. Louis beer in summer months is a circumstance which occasions surprise or agitation in few official breasts.

Least homely of the uses of the caboose, but of necessity a primary one, is that of office for the conductor and supply department for the entire freight crew. The train's operating headquarters is represented by the conductor's desk, among the pigeon holes and filing devices of which that functionary may spend as much as half of the running time of his trip receipting waybills, drawing up his wheel reports, which furnish the basis for the home office's statistical records of all freight and merchandise movement, and doing the other paper work necessary to the orderly conduct of a vast business enterprise.

Lockers, variously located in accordance with the details of the design of the individual hack, but all convenient to the hand of the crew, are provided for the storage of heavy supplies: chains, journal brasses, knuckle pins, rerailing frogs, and wrecking tools for emergencies. Signal fuses, torpedoes, signal flags, lanterns and fuel oil, too, are stored away as neatly and ready to instant use and availability as the signal flags and code books on the bridge of an ocean-going liner. There is also the conductor's emergency air control and in some cases an air horn for calling the attention of the engineer up ahead. This latter device is standard equipment on a number of crummies on the Bangor and Aroostook, while old-timers recall that on some of the western roads where drags were frequently more than a mile long from pilot to markers, caboose roofs mounted fixed-position semaphores for signaling the head end.

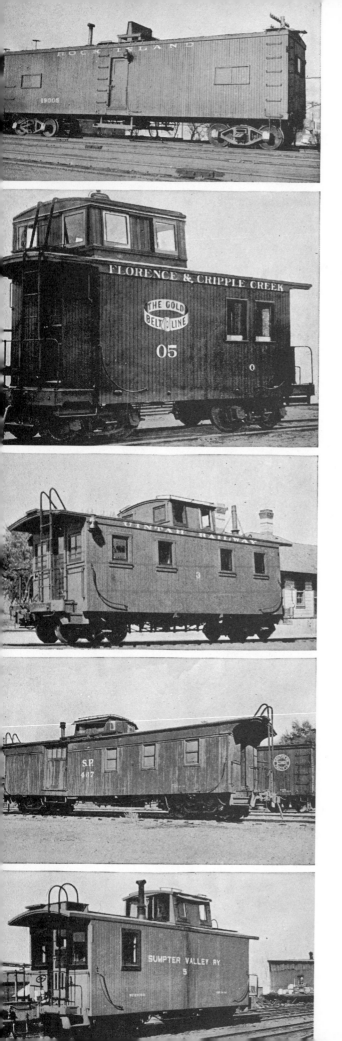

Rock Island high cars with a two-way bench fitted on top are familiar sights around the Chicago yards but not particularly adapted to inclement weather. Photograph by S. P. Davidson.

The once flourishing Florence and Cripple Creek was celebrated as The Gold Belt Line. Its cabooses had enormous cupolas and were numbered in decimals like No. 05 because of their diminutive size. Railroad Magazine photograph.

The motive power of the Uintah Railway was varied and unconventional due to its steep grades and sharp curves, but its crummies followed a conventional pattern as witness No. 3. Photograph by L. J. Ciapponi.

This collector's item was built in the Sacramento shops of the Central Pacific in 1879 with both side doors and cupola and curved platform roofs. It was still in service when Gerald Best discovered it at Keeler, California.

The three-foot-gage cabooses of the Sumpter Valley were distinguished by black trim around their windows against the dark gray of their body paint. L. J. Ciapponi photograph.

The Terminal Railroad Association of St. Louis calls these highly individual cabooses with extra long platforms at either end "shelter cars." In reality they are cabins built on old flat cars. C. W. Witbeck photograph.

These two Missouri-Kansas-Texas crummies of various construction are both painted in the bright yellow and black with which the Katy identifies all its freight equipment and rolling stock. C. M. Clegg photograph.

The Beaver, Meade and Englewood, now owned by the M. K. T., runs lengthwise through the Oklahoma panhandle. Its way car was caught by Preston George at Forgan, Oklahoma.

This ancient Union Pacific caboose, No. 14, saw many years of service over the most famous of all western railroads before it was caught by the camera of C. W. Witbeck.

This historic car, the one time Virginia and Truckee's No. 10, was built by the Kimball Manufacturing Company in San Francisco in 1872. Years later Cecil B. De Mille bought it for one of the properties in Paramount's great money-making film of frontier times, "Union Pacific." Gerald Best photograph.

This Mississippi Export crummie on a siding in Moss Point, Mississippi, is well equipped with gutters to take care of the rain. Railroad Magazine photograph.

This all steel Baltimore and Ohio cabin car is of the modern type which substitutes a bay window rather than a cupola from which members of the crew may survey their train. Railroad Magazine photograph.

Another example of bay window caboose, this time of wooden construction, is this property of the Minneapolis, Northfield and Southern Railroad. Photographed at Randolf, Iowa, by Navarro Fosse.

This Great Northern way car is carefully designed with continuous sheathing extending from the base of the car body clear to the roof of the cupola and lending it a distinguished and unusual appearance. Photographed by Hugh M. Comer.

The Morristown and Erie's beautifully maintained little four-wheel caboose is the delight of its crews even though it seldom travels more than twenty miles in the course of a day's run. Photograph by Lucius Beebe.

In addition to its function as a diner and dormitory for the train crew and a vantage point from which to watch for hot bearings or other operating irregularities, the caboose, in the days before air brakes, was one of the two important braking units of a train, the other being the locomotive and tender. When trains were lighter and hand brakes were standard equipment, it was seldom necessary to tie down more than the crummy and a car or so directly ahead of it and a few cars up forward next the motive power to bring the drag to a stop. To make the braking capacity of the shack more effective than its own light weight would be, it was the custom to load its lockers and spare space with pig iron or old scrap of any description in order to increase its braking effectiveness. This custom, of course, passed into the discard with the universal adoption of the Westinghouse system.

West of the Mississippi—as might be expected, where divisions are longer and cities fewer—cabooses are more than ever self-contained homes for train crews, and Bill Knapke recalls living and eating in a Southern Pacific crummy for a year on end without inconvenience of any sort. In such set-ups a good cook is beyond rubies and many a conductor has been known to ask to have assigned to his run brakemen who were noted more for their ability to run up a creditable tin pan of hot biscuits than for their railroading competence. In the West, too, cabooses are frequently made longer and more on the order of Pullmans to accommodate in folding berths the drovers who, on stock trains, ride to market with their cattle and sheep to assure their arrival in good order. Such elaborate cabooses are usually assigned permanently to a single train crew who spend their own money for their commissary and fittings with the result that shacks sometimes boast such details as radios and elaborate sets of cooking utensils.

One New York, New Haven and Hartford caboose, No. C-246, is famous wherever railroaders foregather for its elaborate collection of more than 200 railroad photographs framed and hung under glass on its walls. The modern streamlined brain cages of the Lehigh Valley are in reality small mobile apartments with electric iceboxes and sponge rubber mattresses on their berths. At one time when an enterprising youth named Robert Willier was handling publicity for the Wabash, he persuaded the management to turn over to him a company way car which he painted a bright Wabash blue of the same tone as the equipment of the road's crack Banner Blue and Bluebird and set up a complete publicity unit with typewriters, mimeograph machines, and other accustomed office equipment. An old wooden four-wheel hack from the Erie, No. 4259, accompanied Lieutenant Robert E. Peary on the trip to the North Pole aboard the *Windward* in 1899 and served the party as sleeping quarters at Etah in the ice fields.

Still another old-time way car to achieve fame was the Virginia & Truckee No. 9 which was repainted with U. P. symbols and numbered the Union Pacific No. 14 for an appearance in Paramount's production, "Union Pacific." It is doubtful if even this car's potential experiences in the frontier days of Flood and Fair and the Comstock Lode could parallel its adventures with the No. 2 company of Cecil DeMille's players and film technicians.

For the shooting of the transparencies or process shots for "Union Pacific," the railroad turned over the trackage and installations of a lonely and seldom used spur running from the main line at Lund, Utah, to Cedar City, a stretch of approximately thirty-five miles of single track rolling up into the grim Utah mountains. The various units of V. & T. power and rolling stock which had been purchased by Paramount and refitted to resemble Union Pacific and Central Pacific equipment of the Golden Spike era of 1869 together with a large company of hired Indians, Hollywood cowboys, directors and cameramen, went up from Los Angeles to do the location shooting against which, as background, the studio work of the principal players would later be filmed.

Although the General Bowker, temporarily disguised with U. P. insignia, was in serviceable order and could work steam, a modern Union Pacific freight locomotive was assigned by President William Jeffers to expedite things and do the heavy work generally.

One cold October morning, while technicians and cameramen were occupied with setting up sound equipment and other details preparatory to shooting some train action, thirty or so film actors, unaccustomed to such rugged scuffles with nature in the raw, foregathered in the ancient hack to play pinochle and otherwise pass the time waiting for their calls.

Courtesy of Railroad Magazine

A TRIO OF LOGGING ROAD CRUMMIES FROM THE PACIFIC COAST

The freight locomotive coupled on the end of No. 14 to haul it up the line and the engineer, unaccustomed to the handling of such ancient and fragile rolling stock, was a little heavy with the throttle. There was a splintering sound and out came the draft gear of No. 14, which, innocent of air brakes, as was all equipment of its period, started gently down the long grade toward Lund and the main, while the freight locomotive, fouled with the broken gear and with its crew in a panic, was impotent to stop it or even follow in pursuit.

The caboose gently accelerated its speed. The engineer leaned on his whistle. Cameramen and executives on the ground screamed futile warnings. The bemused actors inside, accustomed to studio tumults and uproars, continued blandly with their pinochle. Death or at the very least a hideous accident awaited them thirty-five miles down the hills. About the time the caboose was hitting a comfortable fifteen or twenty miles an hour one of the preoccupied mumpers discovered that something was amiss. There didn't seem to be any engine attached to their car and here it was running away downhill at a frightening pace! To the windows, men! To the platforms! For your lives!

Never before or since has there been such a wholesale unloading, as plainsmen and peace officers, Indians, saloon-keepers and Union soldiery kicked out the glass windows and hurled themselves from the platforms onto the frozen Utah right-of-way. In two minutes the car was cleared and amongst the discomforted thespians scattered along a mile of rock ballast broken arms, sprained ankles and battered noggins were a dime a dozen. Blood flowed as at a second Little Big Horn.

The station master at Lund, apprised that trouble was headed his way and at any moment might be expected to go right through the aging fabric of his baggage room, took to the open countryside, having prudently thrown a derail onto the spur to prevent the careening way car from going into the main and, probably, head-on into the Pacific Limited. But a tangent of a mile of level track intervened between the last foothill and the main line and somehow in the confusion of escape one of the now maimed and quivering bit players had contrived to give just enough twist to one of the spavined hand brakes so that the worn shoes grated on the smoking carwheels. The relic of the Sierras ground to a gentle stop twenty feet from the derail. The quaking station agent returned to his post among the telegraphs and glue pots; the battered chivalry of Vine Street was patched up by a U.P. company doctor. The filming was resumed. They might, the actors reflected sadly, just as well have continued their pinochle game and stayed aboard. Probably, however, they would have died of fright and it was just as well they jumped.

If the caboose has figured in legend it has also been written large in the ballad lore of the land. It has probably been dramatized on the stage and it has certainly furnished a favorite theme for several generations of railroad artists and photographers. A complete and definitive monograph on the crummy would probably invoke the learned works of that greatest of all students of American ballads, Professor George Lyman Kittredge of Harvard University, but space forbids the inclusion of any save one fetching jingle penned for his column in the New York *Sun* by the celebrated H. I. Phillips.

THE GLORIFIED CABOOSE

When you hear the freighter whistle
And you see it 'round the bend,
You may nod in high approval
When you view its other end.
Gone the old ramshackle boxcar,
With its flat and noisy wheels,
Gone the car that made the freighter
Look so run down at the heels.

Gone the clatter and the wheezing;
Gone the forlorn aspect, too,
Of the tail end of the freight train
As it rattled out of view.
Now a new caboose shines brightly
At the far end of the train
And she doesn't look like something
Long exposed to wind and rain.

She has lost her look so comic
And her tone so drab and flat;
Now the folk along the railroad
Take a look and gasp, "What's that?"
The caboose has now gone ritzy—
She is like a private car;
She has everything but bathtubs,
Patio and cocktail bar.

Oh, she's now a thing of beauty,
And with pride the train crews burst,
For she helps fulfill the teaching
That the last shall yet be first.
There she goes around the bend, boys—
All dressed up and on the loose!
Oh, what airs the freighter puts on
With a swallowtail caboose!

Be it, however, a swallowtail hack or a less fanciful model, it is probable that the crummy lies nearer to the heart of railroad men everywhere than anything except the wonderful steam locomotives that for many decades have rolled them over the main lines and short hauls, the standard iron and the slim gages of the nation's roads. The all-steel streamlined, airflow shacks of the Peoria Road, the Rock Island and the Erie, and the old-time four-wheel bouncers of the valiant little roads such as the Raritan River and the Morristown and Erie, the doghouses of the stormy mountain divisions of the Rio Grande, conditioned against the winters on the Great Divide, and the buggies of the Santa Fe rolling across the August wheatlands of Kansas, the bright painted way cars of the St. Louis Southwestern rolling south toward the heart of Texas, and the Tuscan red cages of the Pennsy hotshotting through the green fields of Indiana, all have been and still are, most of them, colorful players in the pageant of overland travel by the iron highroad. The saga of the high iron would be the poorer had they never been.

WHISTLE CODE

According to Rule 14 of the Association of American Railroads Standard Code, "o" stands for a short signal blast, "—" for a long.

o Apply brakes. Stop.
— — Release brakes. Proceed.
— o o o Flagman protect rear of train.
— — — — Flagman may return from west or south.
— — — — — Flagman may return from east or north.
o o Answer to any signal not otherwise provided for.
o o o When standing, back; when running, stop at next station.
o o o o Call for signals.
— o o (*Single track.*) To call attention of engine and train crews of trains of the same class, inferior trains and yard engines, and of trains at train-order meeting points, to signals displayed for a following section. If not answered by a train, the train displaying signals must stop and ascertain the cause.
— o o (*Two or more tracks.*) To call attention of engine and train crews of trains of the same class and of inferior trains moving in the same direction and of yard engines, to signals displayed for a following section.
— — o — Approaching public crossings at grade. To be prolonged or repeated until crossing is reached.
————— (very long) Approaching stations, junctions, railroad crossings at grade and where otherwise required.
— — o Approaching meeting or waiting points. (To be sounded one mile before meeting or waiting point.)
o — Inspect train line for leak or for brakes sticking.
o o o o o o Alarm for persons or live stock on track. (This is a succession of short blasts, no given number of signals.)
— o When running against the current of traffic: (1) Approaching stations, curves, or other points where view may be obstructed. (2) Approaching passenger or freight trains and passing freight trains. (3) Preceding the flagman recall signals.
— — — — o Flagman may return from east or north on ...... track.
— — — — o Flagman may return from west or south on ...... track.
— — — — o o Flagman may return from east or north on ...... track.

Lucius Beebe

— — — — o o Flagman may return from west or south on ...... track.
— — — — — o o o Flagman may return from east or north on ...... track.
— — — — o o o Flagman may return from west or south on ...... track.

CONDUCTOR'S SIGNALS

o o When standing, start.
o o When running, stop at once.
o o o When standing, back.
o o o When running, stop at next passenger station.
o o o o When standing, apply or release air brakes.
o o o o When running, reduce speed.
o o o o o When standing, recall flagman.
o o o o o When running, increase speed.
o o o o o o When running, increase train heat.
o — o Shut off train heat.
———— When running, brakes sticking; look back for hand signals.

(3)